UNDER COVER

TO ALL THE AID WORKERS WHO,
LONG AFTER JOURNALISTS HAVE
LEFT WITH THEIR STORY, CHOOSE
TO LIVE, SLEEP AND BREATHE THE
MANY HORRORS IN OUR WORLD.

UNDER COVER

A Duchess and a journalist
bring hope to a million
abandoned children.

BY CHRIS ROGERS
& MARSHALL CORWIN

First published 2010 by Authentic Media.
Milton Keynes.
www.authenticmedia.co.uk

British Library Cataloguing in Publication Data
A catalogue record for this book is available from the British Library.

ISBN: 978-1-85078-858-4

Book design by David McNeill.
www.mrdmcneill.co.uk

Printed and bound in the UK by J F Print Ltd., Sparkford, Somerset.

The identities of some people in this book have been changed for their personal
safety, or to safeguard their work.

CONTENTS

THE FORGOTTEN CHILDREN

The only sound is my footsteps; they echo around the long, narrow corridor. The only light comes through a crack in a boarded window; it pierces the darkness with a single beam. The only smell is urine; it lingers in the musty air and strengthens as I pass a door.

Behind it, an evil secret, kept from the world. As I turn the handle I glance behind me. If I am discovered, I face certain arrest, but I am still alone in the darkness. As the door creaks open it reveals a large, sparse, whitewashed room. A single light bulb flickers above me, revealing a terrible scene of childhood misery.

There are dozens of rows of cots, each one confining a baby or toddler. Their little hands cling to the rusting bars that surround them, their heads rock backwards and forwards, their eyes stare into the empty space above. They are abandoned, unwanted and unloved.

They are imprisoned in their cots for weeks, months, even years. But they do not cry, no matter how lonely, hungry, filthy or sick they become. They quickly learn that their screams are not heard. Nobody comes. They are the forgotten children.

CHRIS ROGERS
Constanta Maternity Hospital, Romania

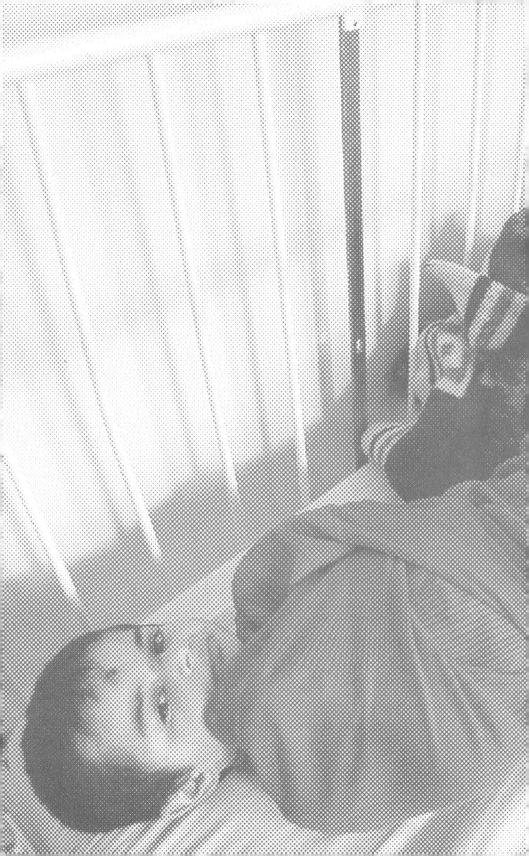

CHAPTER ONE

BY ROYAL APPOINTMENT

It was one of those phone calls you never forget. I was leaving the ITV newsroom on an icy, late November evening in 2007, after the usual non-stop round of filming, editing and meeting deadlines. With the pressure off at last I was looking forward to heading out of London, back to my home in the countryside. Then out of the blue my mobile rang.

'Chris. The boss wants to meet you in half an hour at the Mandarin Hotel in Knightsbridge. Please tell me you can make it!'

I was stunned. It was the personal assistant to Sarah Ferguson, the Duchess of York. 'It's your only chance before she heads back to New York, and you need to bring a DVD of all your Romanian investigations.'

Like several other public figures, the Duchess had previously shown interest in supporting charities highlighted in my reports, but to request a meeting ... ? My mind was racing. If such an influential woman wanted to get more involved, the possibilities were quite staggering. This was an opportunity I couldn't afford to screw up, but I was far from prepared – not to mention miles from Knightsbridge.

I jumped in a cab and called the newsdesk, pleading with an over-worked assistant producer to run off a copy of my reports and bike them to the hotel.

As the taxi weaved through London's West End shopping district, the annual Christmas countdown was already well underway. The streets were packed with shoppers, children tagging along wide-eyed at the twinkling, festive decorations and the stores full of presents. The contrast with my most recent undercover investigation couldn't have been more stark.

A few nights earlier I had been on the streets of Romania, just a two hour flight from London. Posing as a British brothel owner, I had discovered that here it was children themselves who were up for sale on the streets, in the control of gangs of traffickers who offered the 'services' of the youngsters by the hour or, for the right money, even for good. A few miles away I had visited other children living in sewers, huddling by hot water pipes for warmth, many of them sniffing glue. It was ten years since I'd first reported on the scandal of these 'sewer children', and it horrified me that after so long almost nothing seemed to have changed.

In recent years, my reports exposing children's suffering in Eastern Europe had been seen both in Britain on *ITV News* and across the world on CNN. People had been inspired to donate money and, under EU pressure, the countries concerned had on occasion promised improvements. But deep down I knew it was just scratching the surface. Could the woman I was about to meet help take things to a whole new level?

The Duchess is the former wife of the Queen's second son Prince Andrew, the Duke of York. In 1993 she founded the charity Children in Crisis, which helps children caught in conflict or poverty around the world. But as her marriage fell apart in the run-up to her divorce in 1996, the British tabloid press were far more concerned with her alleged affairs, her lifestyle and her weight.

The attacks in the press became ever more personal and abusive and Sarah began to spend increasing amounts of time in the States, away from the endless barrage of negative headlines, establishing a highly successful commercial and media career in a country which seemed to her far less hostile and vindictive.

It was almost too crazy to contemplate, but if I could somehow persuade her to actually take part in an investigation with me, it would be an extraordinary coup. Her global profile would guarantee a commission for a major documentary, which would be snapped up by TV channels worldwide. Filming undercover with the Duchess of York, and possibly even her Royal daughters, would not only be unprecedented, it could have enormous impact – and might just prompt the beginning of the end to the misery of around a million children abandoned without hope across Europe.

The cab was minutes from the Knightsbridge hotel when I suddenly noticed the photo on the front page of the *Metro* newspaper lying on the seat next to me. I had to smile; it was the woman I was about to meet. The Duchess had been snapped with her daughters, Princesses Beatrice and Eugenie, at the previous night's Led Zeppelin concert. They had partied into the small hours with Elvis Presley's former wife Priscilla, her daughter Lisa Marie and grand-daughter Riley. 'Royalty meets Rock 'n' Roll' read the headline.

I began to question my judgment. What would the headlines be for my next investigation? 'Princesses to the rescue of the Paupers'? Perhaps the Duchess of York was just trying to get on the bandwagon, in a cynical attempt to improve her image in Britain. And there was a real danger I'd be accused of selling out to celebrity in order to secure my biggest scoop.

My head was spinning as we pulled up in front of the five-star hotel. Porters in top hats and red tailcoats scurried around me; it felt more than a little ironic that I had come to a place of such grandeur to discuss the plight of some of Europe's poorest children. One thing seemed clear: this meeting was going to be as much about Sarah, Duchess of York selling herself to me, as it was about my pitch to her.

Waiting for me at the hotel entrance was the Duchess's personal assistant, who had called me just half an hour earlier. She hurried me along opulent corridors and through tall double doors where I faced another surprise. It was a huge meeting room with a dozen bottles of mineral water laid out round a boardroom table.

My heart sank. Confronted with such a formal setting, any thoughts of getting the Duchess of York involved in undercover filming suddenly seemed utterly absurd. How could I have let my naïve enthusiasm run away with me? I began to doubt I could even raise such a preposterous idea.

At that moment the Duchess walked into the room. To my amazement, she was followed not by an entourage of charity officials, but by Lisa Marie Presley and her musician husband Michael Lockwood, Lisa Marie's daughter Riley Keogh, and other personal friends and staff.

It was all rather surreal. 'Bloody hell!' I found myself exclaiming. 'I wasn't expecting this kind of audience. Royalty meets Rock 'n' Roll!'

I could not believe I had blurted out the newspaper headline I'd seen in the cab. I prayed for the earth to swallow me up.

But everyone burst into laughter. The ice was broken.

The Duchess seemed to fill the room with her presence. Taking messages from her assistant and holding several other conversations simultaneously, it felt like a whirlwind had swept through. She turned to me to apologise for the delay in getting started: 'Sorry, Chris, things have been rather hectic lately.'

Desperately trying not to stare, I was reduced to the clichéd thought that her pictures did not do her justice.

Lisa Marie Presley was full of cold. She bore a striking resemblance to her legendary father Elvis, and the trademark eyes and lips were also shared by her daughter Riley, a top model. Sniffling away, Lisa Marie explained that she had dragged herself out of bed because the Duchess hadn't stopped talking about the poor children in institutions since my investigations went out, and she was determined to see the reports for herself.

I was starting to feel more relaxed. They had all made a special effort to come here and their concern seemed genuine. Perhaps most tellingly, there was not a photographer or film crew in sight. 'If my mother could only see me now,' I thought. She is a huge Presley fan and a dedicated

Royalist. At last the Duchess brought the meeting to order. 'I hope you don't mind, Chris,' she began, 'but I have brought our friends from America because I think everyone should see your investigations. I know you probably think I am just some ex-Royal who wants to dip her toes in charity work, but when I see something that needs help and I think I can help, then I act, especially when it involves children.'

She was clearly used to addressing people's preconceptions about her motivation, bringing up her work with her new charity 'The Sarah Ferguson Foundation' as part of her defence.

'We work in Africa and countries like Russia, and I do it because I want to, not because I feel I should do. I don't want to do a *Hello!* magazine shoot of me holding abandoned babies. This isn't about me; it's about what I can do. I want to make a difference.'

The Duchess was businesslike and full of energy; I was warming to her by the minute.

'I can show your films to people like the Presleys here and inspire people to donate money,' she continued, 'but we could really go for it and make our own film about this issue of abandoned children and grab everyone's attention. Then we will do something that can really help these children. With the film we create awareness but also inspire people to help us end this awful situation. What do you say?'

I was dumbstruck. As all eyes turned towards me, I finally managed to respond: 'You have taken the words right out of my mouth, Ma'am.' The Duchess smiled and instructed her assistant to play a home video of her recent trip to Albania, showing several orphanages her charity had helped to build. She also described how she had dodged bullets in Liberia to get to villages where many children had lost their parents to disease, famine and war. 'I persuaded the government to allow me to build schools for the children – in other words to give people a fishing rod rather than a fish.'

By now I was completely sold. The image of Sarah Ferguson as portrayed in the media seemed to bear little resemblance to this impassioned individual enthusing about her charity. 'I can work with this woman,' I thought.

The DVD of my reports had fortunately arrived a few minutes earlier, and as I put it in the player, I explained that what they were about to see was not just confined to Romania.

'There are at least a million unwanted children in similar conditions in many other European countries such as Serbia, Turkey, Bulgaria, Hungary and the Czech Republic.'

'Then we'll expose them all,' responded the Duchess.

I sat back as the first of my films began to play to the illustrious gathering, my emotions a heady mix of pride in the journalism, nervousness at how they might react, and a fresh wave of revulsion at the images I now knew so well.

The report opened in a run-down orphanage in southern Romania. Young children were seen tied to beds in filthy conditions. The meeting room fell silent.

For this undercover investigation, cameraman Tony Hemmings and I had posed as charity workers. Once inside the institutions, we found conditions and practices the world believed had been confined to history.

I kept one eye on the screen, the other on the faces of the celebrities and royalty sitting around me. Room after room in the hospital revealed abandoned babies with no future, no family to take them away, no nurses to give them attention. The Presleys began to well up as they watched an abandoned three-week-old girl desperately trying to wrap her tiny lips around the teat of a bottle of milk, left in her crib by nurses who apparently hoped she would somehow feed herself.

In another orphanage, more secret filming showed older children with serious mental and physical disabilities. All were tied up, presumably the simplest option as there were far too few staff to care for them. Believing our cover story that we were charity workers, a nurse grew nervous of what we were witnessing and untied a teenage girl. But the girl immediately started screaming and flailing her arms around. After a moment she put her wrists together and held them out towards the nurse to be tied up again. Even now, I still found the footage harrowing to watch.

The Duchess held her hand over her mouth, her head slowly shaking from side to side.

*

By a strange twist of fate, the journey that brought me to that extraordinary meeting in a Knightsbridge hotel can actually be traced back to the very first report I ever made. Some might even call the whole thing pre-ordained, not least as I had been reporting on a tale of the supernatural.

It was the summer of 1990. Aged fifteen, I was on a school trip to the Yugoslavian village of Medjugorje, famous as the place where six children claimed to see visions of the Virgin Mary. According to the children, she appeared each day at precisely 6.40pm, sometimes in the tower of the local church, at other times on a hillside. As I was a voluntary reporter for a BBC Radio youth programme, I offered to make a feature about the so-called visionaries.

The six children all came from simple peasant families and had understandably become rather wary and elusive, struggling to cope with their celebrity status as millions of pilgrims flooded into the village. Even so, I managed to set up interviews with some of them, and I found my meeting with one boy in particular, the youngest visionary Jacov Colo, quite memorable.

Jacov was just two years older than me, and though he spoke little English, we got on well from the start. We discovered we shared similar tastes in music and, as teenage boys do, we were soon discussing our mutual interest in girls. But I had never met someone close to my age who spoke so openly and easily about his faith.

He was passionate in his belief about receiving the heavenly visits (and also seemed sincere in his hatred of his new-found fame). While unsure of what to make of it all, I nevertheless found it an uplifting and spiritual experience. It was my first insight into the extraordinary lives lived by the most ordinary people and it left a real impression on me.

*

Fifteen years later, in May 2005, something drew me back to Medjugorje. It was approaching the twenty-fifth anniversary of the first sightings of the apparitions, and while my TV work was going well, I was feeling a lack of direction in my life, along with confusion about my own religious beliefs. I took a couple of weeks off work and, to help fund my trip, I landed a commission from *The Times* newspaper to see how the 'Village of Miracles' had changed.

There had of course been a fundamental shift in the intervening years. Yugoslavia had been torn apart by a brutal war involving Bosnians, Croats and Serbs, with tens of thousands killed.

Almost a decade into an uneasy peace, the scars of the war were still evident. Medjugorje was now part of the new country of Bosnia-Herzegovina, and though it hadn't been the scene of any fighting, many local young men had been conscripted into the army, never to return. Hundreds of children had been orphaned, many of them ending up in care.

I was surprised and disappointed at how commercialised Medjugorje had become. By now it had grown into a small town, and around twenty-five million pilgrims were said to have visited, making it one of Europe's most unlikely top tourist destinations. It boasted hotels, restaurants and souvenir shops selling plastic statues of the Virgin Mary and other kitsch religious merchandise.

Like many towns in Bosnia-Herzegovina, Medjugorje nestles in a valley, surrounded by mountains. I decided to take a hike above the main town, away from the tacky religious 'Costa del Sol'. As I watched the sun rise over the breathtaking landscape, I began at last to feel the sense of peace I had experienced on my first visit all that time ago.

I was desperate to find Jacov, but making contact with him wasn't easy. The visionaries had steadfastly insisted over twenty-five years that they were neither suffering from delusions nor taking part in some elaborate hoax, and officials in the town seemed keener than ever to protect them from journalists.

But eventually I succeeded in tracking him down and, to my relief, he greeted me like a long-lost friend, rather than a prying reporter. He was now a family man with three children, and he still talked with passion and conviction about his daily divine visits. 'When I see Our Lady she's like a normal person. I talk to her like I'm talking to you, and sometimes I can touch her. I used to get so angry because people didn't believe me,' he added, 'but now I just pray for them.'

Even after so long, I found it all completely perplexing; he talked about the unbelievable as if it were the most natural thing in the world. I noticed a statue of the Virgin Mary in his garden and wondered if it was similar to his apparitions.

'No way!' he laughed. 'My wife bought that statue, so who am I to argue? Our Lady is so beautiful it's hard to find the words to describe what she looks like.'

Jacov's three children captured his attention for a moment as they came screaming into the garden, chasing the family dogs. His mood suddenly changed, as if the children had prompted a disturbing memory. After a long pause, he asked if I and Matt Writtle, the photographer I was travelling with, would do him a favour: 'I want to show you something which has shocked me.'

He explained that he had discovered a neglected orphanage near the Bosnian capital Sarajevo. Perhaps we might take some photos which he could show to pilgrims to help raise much-needed funds?

'If you are willing, I will take you there. The children desperately need help.'

I knew Jacov was orphaned himself, so if nothing else I felt it was worth the six hour round trip to get an extra insight into his unusual life for my *Times* article. But I was also keen to find out what exactly it was that he found so disturbing.

As we sped through the rugged mountain scenery, reminders of the terrible war were everywhere. Few of the villages we passed were untouched. Houses were peppered with bullet holes, some of them still without roofs. And as we got closer to Sarajevo, the landscape became littered with completely bombed-out buildings. For the first time, I was getting a true sense of the awful reality of the Bosnian war.

Jacov told us that the institution he was taking us to was full of children orphaned or abandoned during the war. I had never actually been to an orphanage and was unsure what to expect, but I began to fear that it wouldn't be good.

As we entered the outskirts of Sarajevo, I noticed queues of families gathering outside what looked like an air-raid shelter, its pock-marked walls witness to ferocious fighting in the war.

'That's now a feeding centre for thousands of homeless families,' Jacov informed me. 'Little has changed in the ten years since the end of the war. Sarajevo is a city still scarred and struggling to move on.'

We turned into a long drive strewn with rubbish. At the end of it was a bleak, grey building which could easily have been mistaken for another ruin. Half its roof was missing and the concrete walls had cracks so huge you could see through them. Two tired-looking nurses and a doctor dressed in a tatty white coat were at the doorway to greet us. Jacov had clearly been here many times; they embraced him warmly.

The doctor stretched out to shake my hand, introducing himself as Zihad Korjenic, the chief social worker. 'Are you prepared for this?' he asked gently.

'Prepared for what?' I wondered, casting Matt a glance.

At this point our interpreter, a mother of three, shook her head and said to me apologetically: 'I can't do this, Chris. I'm going to stay outside.'

Dr Zihad gestured towards the doorway. 'Before you go inside, I want you to know we are good people. We do everything we can for our patients. But it isn't much.'

As he opened the door, I was overwhelmed by the stench, a powerful, musty odour of urine and sweat. It was all I could do not to retch.

'You will get used to it, I promise,' Jacov whispered to me. I walked down a long corridor, its bare walls stained yellow from tobacco smoke. It led to a dozen small rooms. I poked my head round the door of the first one and couldn't believe what I saw. Lying across just three beds were fourteen children, aged from about eight to fifteen. They were tucked up next to several emaciated old men and women. The sheets were stained with excrement and sweat and, though it was boiling out-side, the windows were shut.

I was speechless. Eventually, I managed to ask Dr Zihad: 'Why are there adults here?'

'They came here as children around fifty years ago and have never left,' he answered. 'Their families have never come to see them since. They have nowhere to go.'

Each face, young or old, was emotionless. I smiled and waved 'Hello', but there was no reaction. In the corner, a TV was showing some sort of game show. Applause and laughter echoed round the sparse room, but neither the children nor the adults paid any attention. Some of them lay on their beds staring at the ceiling, seemingly unaware of anything else around them. Others, tied to cheap plastic chairs, rocked backwards and forwards.

'They rock to comfort themselves. We just don't have the staff to give them attention,' explained Dr Zihad. 'It's heartbreaking.'

I was utterly unprepared for suffering and neglect on this scale and struggled to hold myself together.

Dr Zihad reeled off a shopping list of resources the orphanage urgently required: 'We need the basics – food, underwear, shoes and medicine – before we can even begin to think about specialist equipment. We want to separate the children from the adults but we do not have enough space. We need a new building and then we can move the patients and give them proper therapy. All we can offer them right now is love – when we have time.'

At that moment, one of the children screamed out 'Mama!' A nurse rushed into the room, scooped the child up and placed her on the concrete floor, yanking down her trousers at the same time. Urine splashed all around her.

'The children always call me Mama,' explained the nurse. 'They never make it to the toilet – not that it works anyway – so I have to stop them peeing on the beds. This is the only way.'

I was witnessing the most unimaginable, undignified existence. As the staff themselves acknowledged, this was not an orphanage. It was a building full of dying rooms.

And each room revealed more horrific suffering. Jacov took me into one area crammed with cots, containing not babies but teenagers tied to the rusting bars with pieces of cloth. All were staring at the blank walls in silence.

'These children were abandoned by their parents because they could not afford to take care of them. They are all severely physically and mentally disabled.'

I am no expert, but it seemed clear that most of the children's disabilities had been made worse by the years of sub-human treatment. I stroked the face of a ten-year-old called Mina and she smiled back. But a hug was impossible. A bandage had been wrapped around her waist pinning her arms behind her back. Her feet were tied to the end of the cot.

When I asked Dr Zihad why she was restrained so severely, he explained that she desperately needed therapy. 'She has waves of aggression and bites off chunks of skin from her own body.' Mina's face was covered with painful-looking scars and her entire body was bruised.

Another girl was sitting up in bed, with just her legs bound together. In the midst of this living hell, it was her story that finally caused me to break down. The nurse told me that for just a few minutes each day they untied her arms so she could read a postcard from her parents. The postcard had been delivered to the orphanage ten years earlier, the only one she had ever received.

I watched Jacov trying to get a smile out of the children, stroking their faces and hands and pulling silly faces. It struck me that, as an orphan himself, this was intensely personal for him. Had his relatives not taken him in, he could easily have ended up in a place like this.

*

When my article appeared in *The Times*, the reaction was phenomenal. Many readers sent donations to a local charity in Sarajevo, and conditions at the orphanage soon began to improve. Jacov phoned me in London to say they'd just taken delivery of a truckload of therapy equipment, and Dr Zihad even got his new building so he could at last separate children from adults.

Back in the ITV newsroom I felt reinvigorated. Not only was there the satisfaction of feeling 'job done', I now had my sense of direction. I would try to focus my future TV career on exposing injustice and human suffering around the world, especially where children were involved.

But it was all about to happen far more quickly than I could possibly have imagined. A call came through to the newsroom from a small human rights organisation called Mental Disability Rights International, based in Washington DC. Its director, Eric Rosenthal, had seen my article in *The Times* about the Sarajevo orphanage and called to tell me that what I had uncovered was, in his view, just the tip of the iceberg.

'If you can pull it off, I suggest you head to Romania,' he advised me. 'People think the problems there are over, but they are simply covered up. It won't be easy and you'll have to go undercover, but multiply what you found in Sarajevo by about two hundred and you'll be close to the scale of the problem there.'

It was a phone call that would lead to a host of undercover investigations over the next three years. I would discover that more than a million children are being held in inhumane conditions across Europe. There would be death threats from gangsters, and acts of intimidation and slander from government ministers and secret police.

I would gather help from aid workers, doctors and politicians, and then finally from a duchess and her princesses.

CHAPTER TWO

ABANDONED WITHOUT HOPE

The ITV newsroom was buzzing. With just minutes to go to the evening news, stories were breaking and stressed correspondents were still editing their reports. Journalists like me thrive on that creative chaos, but for once I was not a part of it.

I had managed to persuade the editor, Deborah Turness, to give me a few days off from the daily reporting rota to research a possible investigation into Romania's orphanages. She knew that if it came off it would be a huge scoop, as Romania was just a few months from being officially accepted into the European Union.

But my only lead was the phone call from Eric Rosenthal at Mental Disability Rights International. Checking out the MDRI website, it appeared to be a small American charity which lobbied for better treatment of the mentally and physically ill. Made up of former journalists and doctors, it compiled reports on care systems (or the lack of them) in countries throughout the world, using evidence from charity workers and other personnel. In its archives I found a damning report on Romania's institutions, much as Eric had outlined to me.

There were, however, several key problems. Not only were all the report's contributors anonymous, the Romanian authorities had branded the MDRI report misleading and out of date, stating that such places had been 'dealt with'.

Eric had warned me about Romania's propaganda machine, insisting that the ill-treatment of unwanted Romanian children still went on: 'Not a penny has been invested. The abuse continues, hidden from the outside world, in institutions where foreign journalists and EU inspectors are never taken, because their care falls well below EU standards.' He also advised me that his contacts in the country would not help me, as they would be too scared of the consequences.

'Brilliant,' I thought, 'that makes this investigation impossible.' But on the old journalistic principle that if a story's easy to find, then it's probably not much of a story, I decided to hit the phones anyway.

I spent day after day working through the dozens of charities operating in Romania, which remained one of Europe's poorest countries. Not one of them stood up Eric's claims. And not one of their websites mentioned dirty institutions or any kind of human suffering. Instead, staring up at me were the happy faces of children being cared for in special homes, often built by the charities involved.

This is an extract from my reporter's notes during that period, the conversation with an aid worker from a well-known Romanian charity typical of the many I had:

Is it true that abandonment of babies is still a problem?
Some children are still given up by their mothers
— too poor to care for them — but only in poor
gypsy Roma communities. Most are sick and need
special care.

How many?
About 500 abandoned each year by very poor parents.

So where do they go?
No large institutions for children — shut
down. And by law children under 3 cannot be
institutionalised. Small State or charity-run
care homes for sick or unwanted children over 3

— but most go to Romanian families — paid to look
after children. If you come here you will not find
children in bad conditions like years ago — that
is old news.

So what does your charity do?
We help unwanted children find foster parents
through the authorities. Also look after children
abandoned 15 or 20 years ago — they need help
as they become adults. Some need to find a job,
education, a home, others need special care —
thousands have HIV or Aids from dirty needles
used in orphanages twenty years ago — but everyone
knows that story. There's no story for you here if
looking for abandoned children like those filmed by
journalists after the fall of communism.

I knew only too well the shocking images she referred to. They were all over our TV screens in the early nineties after the fall of the dictator Nicolae Ceausescu: abandoned, half-starved Romanian children left to rot in dirty, inhumane institutions.

For a quarter of a century, Ceausescu ruled Romania with an iron fist, combining communist principles with extravagant, ill-thought out schemes which all but bankrupted the country. He decided early on that a key priority was to create a larger national labour force to help the country work its way to greater prosperity, imposing a strict ban on abortions and contraception to increase the birthrate. Couples who failed to have children by the age of twenty-five faced extra taxes.

But Ceausescu was increasingly out of touch with the reality of the hardship caused by his incompetence. Romania slid towards financial ruin, with much of the population close to starvation. Many families couldn't afford to feed the children they had been pressured to conceive, opting instead to abandon them to State institutions.

By late 1989, even the feared Romanian security forces couldn't prevent mass demonstrations against Ceausescu's totalitarian rule. In just a few days, the unthinkable happened: his authority crumbled, the army turned against him and, over Christmas, he and his wife Elena were executed by a firing squad.

I remember the scenes on television as foreign news crews took their first steps behind Romania's Iron Curtain. Extreme poverty and the scars of a bloody revolution were no great surprise, but nothing could prepare the world for what was found in Romania's orphanages. More than a hundred thousand babies and children were crammed into small rooms, unwanted and unloved. They rocked backwards and forwards to comfort themselves. Most were starving and showing the physical and mental signs of institutionalisation. Many had skeletal bodies and had harmed themselves, either by banging their heads against concrete walls or scratching their skin. Some were injured so severely that staff had tied them to their beds to stop them inflicting any more self-harm.

Most were not orphans. Their parents had abandoned them, hoping that at the very least they would be fed and would sleep with a roof over their heads. But the impoverished State system was completely overwhelmed.

The world reacted with a flood of donations and aid. Charities swooped in to improve the conditions of dilapidated orphanages. Hundreds of foreign families filed for adoption, offering a new life for Romania's children. The most famous appeal in Britain was by the BBC TV children's programme *Blue Peter*, which raised more than six million pounds to build a series of smaller orphanages. The aim was to create a healthy, family-like environment and each home had a bronze plaque attached to the door with an engraved message: 'A present from the children of Britain'.

Nearly twenty years later, my research began to convince me that things really had continued to change for the better. It certainly made sense, I told myself, as providing adequate child welfare was a condition of Romania's imminent entry to the European Union. After what I had witnessed in the orphanage in Sarajevo a few months earlier, I was actually feeling very relieved that other children were not suffering a similar fate.

But the journalist in me was dreading having to tell my editor that the story did not stand up after all. Time was running out and soon I would go back to the daily reporting roster. I had no idea what to do next to try to take the investigation forward. I looked at the flashing cursor on my blank computer screen for what seemed like hours.

Just as I packed my bag to head home, my mobile phone rang. It was the aid worker from a Romanian charity I had called a few days earlier. In broken English she asked me if I was still planning to come to Romania to make a film. I explained how I was close to ruling it out as a story.

'Listen to me,' she whispered urgently. 'Some of what I said to you wasn't true, but charities are too frightened to help journalists.'

She was clearly very nervous herself. 'We are under strict instructions not to allow journalists or cameras into the institutions, otherwise our projects will be shut down. Foreign charities have been threatened that they will be kicked out of the country if they help journalists. The authorities can quickly discredit and disgrace a charity with clever lies. They can shut you down with a click of a finger.'

I scrambled for my pen and reporter's notebook. 'I understand. Tell me what you can – I can promise you I don't reveal my sources.'

'There are some improvements in Romania,' she told me. 'The best work is by charities that have set up their own homes to look after unwanted children. European Union money has been used to build the new smaller State institutions I told you about when we last spoke. It's these good, well-funded homes that the EU inspectors see, but there are still many problems. Even some of the new State homes lack decent care, and as for the old ones, well, they are terrible. They should have been closed down years ago – but they haven't.'

'What about abandonment?' I asked, aware she could hang up on me at any time. 'Is it still a big problem?'

'Many children are still abandoned, thousands a year, but the government insists the number is only around five hundred. They are hidden in the hospitals and institutions that are officially closed. There are not enough foster parents to take on unwanted children and the government is overwhelmed.

'Please come here and expose it,' she pleaded. 'Many aid workers are given access to the hospitals holding abandoned babies and the institutions, old and new, but I cannot help you any more. Keep calling around and perhaps someone will be brave enough to help you. Good luck.'

Then the phone went dead.

I quickly found her number and called her straight back – but there was no answer. As I hung up, my phone immediately rang again. 'Thanks for calling back,' I said with some relief. 'I just need to ask you a few more questions … '

But it wasn't the charity worker. The voice on the other end of the line was English and male. In a calm and educated voice he said: 'I represent the interests of Romania and its people.'

At first I thought it was a joker in the newsroom. I scanned the sea of desks around me. *ITV News* was on the air and everyone was simply too busy to be playing practical jokes.

Then the caller issued a direct and chilling threat: 'We were warned journalists like you might try to discredit Romania's eligibility to enter the EU. My warning to you is to watch your back if you come here. We are very sensitive to anyone who gets in the way of our ambitions. You are not welcome in Romania, Mr Rogers. We know your address, your history and who you are. There is no story for you here – do you understand what I am saying?'

I demanded to know who was speaking, but the voice continued smoothly: 'It's not important who I am. Yes, I am British, but I work for the Romanian State and we are concerned that you are asking too many of the wrong questions. It's my job to warn you against calling people here and asking for information about how Romania's children are cared for. They will not help you. You are wasting your time. Everything is fine here. Find another story that actually exists.'

Then he hung up.

I had certainly rattled a cage, but his threats only served to encourage me, especially now I knew that charities were being intimidated to conceal the truth.

I had finally scribbled something that looked like a story in my reporter's notes:

- Threatening phone call

- Perhaps from Romania's more thug-like version
  of a government spin doctor

- Told to watch my back and no story for you
  in Romania

- Foreign charities obviously under strict
  instructions not to co-operate with
  journalists. Maybe they want to expose what is
  going on but would not dare risk being booted
  out of the country. Romanian charities are
  either just as scared of being shut down or too

```
damned proud to discredit their country. May
even be co-operating with authorities.

· Perhaps some charity informed authorities
  about me?

· Some kind of cover-up by aid workers who have
  access to the worst institutions
```

I looked again at that last sentence in my notes, repeatedly underlining it with my pen. It was staring me in the face. I would have to become an aid worker to get access.

*

It would take many months to create a decent 'cover' and gather help for the investigation. In a painfully slow process, I set up a website for a bogus charity, filling the pages of the site with pictures and literature about a donation-and-grant programme for projects. Claiming the 'charity' wanted to donate large sums of money, I wrote on headed paper to the Romanian authorities asking if we could work voluntarily in their institutions and look at possible projects for donations. The red tape was immense but eventually the breakthrough came: I was offered a voluntary work placement for my cameraman and myself. It was at one of Romania's most modern, show-piece institutions, so might well not harbour the terrible conditions I had been told about, but it was a start.

Simultaneously, I continued to call charities operating in Romania, concentrating this time only on international organisations based outside the country. My persistence paid off and a few aid workers finally agreed to help. Under my false identity as a fellow charity aid worker, a Canadian volunteer said she would sneak me into a large orphanage where she claimed to have witnessed appalling care. British and American aid workers would show me round maternity hospitals which they said were overflowing with abandoned babies.

It was August 2006, just a few months before Romania's entry to the EU, when I touched down undercover in Bucharest with my cameraman Tony Hemmings. We each had aid worker IDs along with fake charity brochures, money for bribes and, if months of meticulous work paid off, access to institutions Romania would rather we didn't see.

Both of us had been to Romania before. Ten years earlier, I'd reported on the country's street-children for the BBC, and Tony was one of the first foreign cameramen to enter the country during the revolution. For each of us, the transition from wrecked East European State to prospective European Union member was astonishing.

Bucharest was once a grey, dirty city without a soul. Like many capitals under the communist system, the streets were drab, with few bars and restaurants. Queues for food at the supermarkets and bakeries were endless. The pavements were lined with children begging and women so desperate they risked certain arrest by prostituting themselves.

Most nights the electricity failed and the city was plunged into an eerie darkness. People were too poor to venture outdoors. The only sign of life came from the many factories that poured pollution into the sky, often leaving the city cloaked in choking smog.

As Tony and I headed by taxi into the city centre, it was hard to believe we were looking at the same country. Tony pointed out squares and streets which had seen fierce fighting during the revolution. Now those same areas were peppered with bars and strip clubs. Neon lights advertising Coca Cola and Nike trainers cast a multi-coloured glow across Revolution Square, where Ceausescu had looked on in bewilderment at a nation that had turned against him. The empty shops where hungry families once waited for days for bread had been replaced with McDonald's, Burger King and even a Hard Rock Cafe. Crumbling blocks of flats had been demolished, making way for tall modern office buildings and five star hotels.

The enormous Ceausescu Palace still dominated the city skyline, but was now home to the Romanian Parliament. Democracy and foreign investment had transformed one of Europe's poorest countries into its fastest-growing. The Romanian government proudly declared that the country had met all the conditions set for European Union membership, with corruption under control and 'the best child welfare system in Europe'. After years of monitoring Romania's progress, the EU had overwhelmingly agreed to raise the Romanian flag in Brussels in just a few weeks' time.

I turned to Tony with some concern as the taxi pulled up at our lavish hotel. I was finding it hard to believe that the story we had come to film could possibly exist.

'If it does, Chris, then the very fact Romania is so westernised and developed makes it all the more important that you find the story.'

Tony was right. There was little excuse for human suffering in a country that had clearly had huge amounts of money injected into its veins.

I was very glad Tony had been appointed my cameraman. This was not our first investigation together and our adventures had made us close friends. But, more importantly, he is one of the best. He has vast experience, having filmed dozens of wars and historic events. Over the next few days, we would have to pretend to be aid workers from a bogus charity. It was well beyond Tony's job description, but I knew he would be more than willing to go the extra mile, whatever the dangers, to try to find the story.

Our hotel was in a prime position overlooking the grand Parliament buildings, and our investigation began just a few blocks away. My

Canadian contact, Tanya, worked at an institution called Marin Pazon in central Bucharest, a so-called 'Centre for Rehabilitation' for children between the ages of four and eighteen.

By helping us, Tanya knew she might be thrown out of the country, but she'd told me it was a risk she was prepared to take, as she was so frustrated and overwhelmed by what she had witnessed. Together, we had devised a plan to try to protect her. A few weeks before arrival, I sent her a written request from my bogus charity to see her place of work, explaining that we were 'looking for institutions which urgently need an injection of funds'. She showed the letter to the director of Marin Pazon, who granted us permission to visit.

Now, with fake IDs and a hidden camera disguised as a button on Tony's shirt, we finally made our way there. From the outside, the two-storey building was unremarkable, hidden at the end of a back street. It had a flat roof with windows covered in metal bars. Tony gave me the thumbs-up to signal he was recording on his hidden camera.

Tanya was waiting for us at the main gates, a young student-type, probably in Romania on a gap year. The atmosphere was tense; there were no hugs or hellos and she appeared nervous.

I tried to reassure her: 'You have the letters I sent to prove you thought we were a real charity, so don't worry – we won't tell anyone you helped us knowingly.'

She shrugged her shoulders. 'I will lose my job here when this comes out anyway. I just feel your film will do more good for these children than I can.'

As she led us up the driveway towards the entrance of the building, she told us that the director of the institute had left to go home – there were just a couple of night staff remaining. 'This is your best chance to get away with it. The director's quite clued up when it comes to journalists, but the nurses won't care what you're up to. You can bribe them if you have to.'

As we approached the main doors I took a deep breath. It was the culmination of months of work. Would everything I'd heard turn out to be true, or nothing more than well-intentioned exaggeration? Little did I know that what I was about to find would be so shocking, it would later move a duchess and two princesses to contact me and get involved themselves.

Tanya swung open the doors and a familiar smell filled the air. It was the same odour I'd first experienced at the orphanage in Sarajevo all those months ago, a highly unpleasant mix of urine and sweat.

But it wasn't just the smell; as we were ushered into a large, sparsely-decorated room, we were hit by a deafening wall of sound. More than a hundred children were screaming and crying, punching each other and throwing themselves around. Wherever I looked, children rocked themselves violently. Others stood banging their heads repeatedly against the dirty, concrete walls.

Several had their hands tied behind their backs, seemingly the only way the overworked nurses could try to stop them hurting themselves. But it had little effect. Almost every child was covered in bruises and scars, clearly visible through tattered clothing. Many were almost naked. Some had nappies overflowing with excrement and covered in flies.

Tony and I were overwhelmed by what we were seeing. Shouting above the noise, Tanya explained: 'The children in this institute receive little or no medication to calm them down. It's always like this.'

Her tone was very matter of fact. After months working here, she had inevitably had to harden herself to the distressing sight of near-naked children throwing themselves around the room.

'They were abandoned at birth. Some were born with mental health problems, but many arrived in need of little more than a bit of attention. Their condition just gets worse here. All I can do is help the nurses feed them and put them to bed – there are no other resources.'

All the children were deeply scarred by this indescribable place. We should have been an interesting interruption to their hellish lives, but most were too traumatised to care. The few who noticed us looked up through dulled eyes, staring out of dirty, bruised faces.

I could tell that Tony was getting frustrated: the trouble with hidden cameras is that you have no idea what images – if any – you are capturing.

One of the two nurses in the room rushed towards us, asking who we were. We handed over our fake aid worker IDs and Tanya explained we had permission to be here. Tony took the opportunity to ask the nurse if he could film the room to show people back home how much help was needed. She nodded wearily and threw her hands in the air in exasperation. 'Film it all! I'm tired of hiding my country's problems.'

Tony pulled a small home video camera out of his pocket and began to film the disturbing scenes all around us. I turned to the nurse and asked if they had any facilities to give the children therapy.

'We have nothing – only beds and this room. We place the children on the rug and the benches and they stay here until bedtime. We feed them, of course, but I wouldn't suggest you join us for that. They are like animals.'

As we talked, the other nurse stood in the middle of the mayhem, unable to cope. A girl punched her in the back and she swung round and hit the child in the face.

I spotted a young boy cowering in the corner. He was desperately thin and his tongue hung from his mouth. He was the only child who didn't rock or run riot in the room. The nurse told me he couldn't walk or talk because he'd never been taught to. When I got closer, I noticed his hands and feet were tied to the wall. A tear crept out of a bruised eye. When I asked the nurses for his name, they said they didn't know it.

A few moments later, the children were marched to their beds, some of them even being dragged along the floor. In the chaos, one of the nurses noticed we were still filming and told us to stop. She appeared to be getting suspicious and demanded we hand over the tape. We refused and quickly escaped before her temper rose further.

Journalism is a funny old business. As Tony and I drove away, we couldn't help feeling jubilant at finding the story so quickly, discussing enthusiastically what we might have on tape and the impact it would have back home. It was only when we got back to the hotel that our personal feelings of nausea and revulsion kicked in. We fell into a long silence, trying to come to terms with what we had just witnessed. But disturbing as it was, Marin Pazon was just one institution. We still had a lot of work to do if we were to prove it was not an isolated case.

Finding other orphanages like Marin Pazon would not be easy. None of our other aid worker contacts worked in a similar institution. We were on our own.

*

During my research, one name had come up time and again. Negra Voda was an old institution, notorious for its medieval standard of care. It was time to hit the road, accompanied by a translator from an American charity who had agreed to help us.

Negra Voda was a six hour drive from Bucharest. As we drove into the car park, a pack of dogs wandered out of the entrance, followed by a tired-looking man. We handed over our false ID cards, peddling our yarn that we were a charity looking for places which needed help. The man shrugged his shoulders, explaining that the institute had been shut down just a few weeks earlier.

He told us it once held more than a hundred teenagers, most of them disabled, but now only six children were left, awaiting their placements elsewhere. Could it be a sign that Romania was, after all, closing down its worst institutions? I asked him where all the other children had gone. 'Some are in a better place in new EU-funded care homes, but most of the older ones were moved to Techirghiol, ten miles from here.'

He shook his head as he said it, and we were about to find out why. Located off a main road on a dirt track, the Techirghiol Centre for Recuperation and Rehabilitation was a long-term adult institution. It looked like an open prison. A huge cage surrounded the main building and every window was barred. A limping man dressed in a white medical uniform took us to his office, where once again we promoted our fictitious charity work. He turned out to be the institute's director, and I handed him one of our bogus pamphlets which explained how the 'charity' operated and how we supposedly raised our funds.

By now Tony was in full character, spouting forth about how we had issued grants to a number of projects in Romania to improve facilities, and how we could provide medicine and even volunteers. After an hour of tall stories and several thick Romanian espressos, we seemed to have won his trust.

'We receive very little money from the authorities,' he said. 'We would welcome any help. There are just three doctors here, including myself. The institute has the capacity for two hundred patients. Two years ago we had two hundred and twenty; now we have more than four hundred. They keep bringing them here from all over Romania, even though they know we have no more room.'

I started to feel sorry for him. He seemed exhausted and his face had an expression of weary resignation. He looked me in the eye as he said: 'I'll take you inside to show you around, but I warn you it is very disturbing.'

In the courtyard, a teenager in a baseball cap grabbed my arm. 'Are you here to help us? Please come and help us!' he shouted.

He wouldn't let go of me until I walked through the net curtain at the entrance to one of three huge buildings. He clearly didn't want to follow us in. Inside, the floorboards creaked and the walls crumbled when we touched them. Able bodies with disturbed minds wandered freely in the corridors. Many tugged our hands or tried to hold onto us.

I poked my head into the first room. It was tiny. Five beds took up every inch of space. 'These rooms are built for two beds, but we are over-crowded. What can I do?' said the director in exasperation.

An elderly woman lay like a bundle of wrinkled skin at the top end of her bed. She was naked. Room after room exposed the human misery of the young and the very old. Age or sex didn't matter here; men, women, teenage boys and girls lay motionless, some two to a bed. They only moved to flick away the flies from their shaven heads.

The face of a girl who looked about seventeen appeared from behind some yellow covers. She began to scream and moan. The director ushered me away explaining: 'She has just got here and is still getting used to it.'

There were just two lavatories with broken seats serving the four hundred patients. The director showed me his medicine cabinet which was almost empty. 'We have enough supplies for five more days, but only if we save it for the most urgent cases,' he said.

A skeletal boy appeared, saliva pouring from his mouth. His legs were so thin he could barely walk. Called Marios, he was naked from the waist down. He was at most eighteen, probably much younger, and he shared a bed with another disturbingly thin boy whose name nobody knew. With great difficulty Marios pulled himself onto the bed. He was trying to say something, his hand grasping mine.

'He can't talk; he hasn't learned how to,' said the director. 'This is what life in an institution does to humans.'

There were sores on the boys' legs and backsides, with pus pouring out of them. As they turned to ease the pain, I could hear their bones creaking. It was as much as I could take. This adult institution was the final resting place for Romania's abandoned, and it was like something out of a Nazi concentration camp. As I tried to reach fresh air, the director grabbed me. 'Please understand I am not the creator of this situation. This is Romania, my friend.'

*

The international community had bought into Romania's propaganda that the government had tackled the issue and closed down the worst orphanages. It was easy to understand why: some of the most infamous institutions had indeed been shut and replaced by new, smaller family-style homes, which were all outsiders ever got to see.

These smaller homes held ten to fifteen children, cared for by two workers. My aid worker contacts called them the 'show-homes', the places where EU inspectors, fund-raisers and celebrities were taken on official visits. It was in one of them, in the town of Oradea in the northwest of the country, where Tony and I had been granted temporary volunteer work.

But the aid workers told me that, behind the gloss, even these institutions had disturbing practices. They were certain we would find the evidence if, unlike the VIP visitors, we were able to spend a full twenty-four hours working as helpers.

From the outside, our care home looked like a cheaply-built bungalow circled by a high metal fence. It was one of a row of ten similar homes lining a street in a suburban area of the town. Inside, the brightly-decorated rooms smelt clean and new and were filled with Ikea-style furniture. The atmosphere was calm, in contrast to the chaos we had witnessed in the Marin Pazon institute.

Our first chore was to help with supper for ten children in the kitchen. Some were able to feed themselves but others clearly needed a hand. I sat next to a young girl and began to feed her some broth. I stroked her face to try and get a smile but she didn't flinch or even look at me, staring blankly at the ceiling as the broth dribbled back out of her mouth.

Then, a care worker pointed to the bedrooms and told me to take food to some other children. Inside the first bedroom I found fourteen-year-old David. He was lying in his bed wide awake, his head rocking aggressively. He was trying to bang his foot against a wall covered in large holes that he must have created, but something was stopping his foot from moving. I pulled back his covers; his hands and feet had been tied to the bedposts with scarves to stop him causing any more damage.

In another room, fifteen-year-old Simona had been strapped to a chair for the entire day. When I asked what was wrong with her, the care worker explained that she was blind and was tied up for her own safety. Another girl, Marion, had tape wrapped around her head to break her falls as she tried desperately to walk. Her feet were twisted and useless from lack of exercise. Other children murmured and dragged themselves around the room like teenage babies.

Over a hundred children and twenty staff had recently been moved into the complex of new homes in Oradea, following the closure of a huge Ceausescu-built institute which had been condemned by European Union inspectors.

While the new buildings were certainly much nicer and the staff ratios better, it seemed old habits died hard. The physical restraint of children is utterly prohibited under international law. We were desperate to document what was happening, but we had a problem: the hidden camera was not working.

So I kept the two care workers talking in the kitchen while Tony wandered around the home filming on the small video camera. When the care workers went back to their tasks, I kept a close eye on them and called Tony's mobile, pretending to speak to my family back home. If the coast was still clear to film, I would let him know in a coded conversation: 'Ah, so you're on your own. I see. No one's coming to see you today. Well why don't you crack on with your work?'

Or I would warn him by saying: 'You have to go, do you? Someone is coming to see you now? OK, well I'll leave you as you have company.'

It worked. Tony managed to film all the disturbing scenes of children tied up and left in their beds all day. We were told to report back the next morning but we had all the footage we needed.

There was a final, crucial piece of the gruesome jigsaw puzzle still to put into place. The root of the whole problem, the abandonment of babies, was still by all accounts a significant issue, and I was anxious to see what was happening to these youngest victims of all. Legislation introduced in order to gain entry into the EU stated that no infant under three could be placed in any institution unless he or she was 'severely disabled'. Instead, children abandoned in maternity hospitals were supposed to be sent to local foster families or returned to relatives. The Romanian government, keen to show it could care for its orphans, had banned international adoption. But was its fostering programme succeeding in saving newly-borns from the trauma of institutionalisation?

Our first port of call was the Black Sea resort of Constanta, which bills itself as the Eastern gateway of Europe. The ancient city is popular with young, wealthy Romanians for its beaches, night clubs and casinos. But our interest lay elsewhere: we were heading for its maternity hospital. We did not have permission to visit its wards and we had not even asked; we knew we would not be allowed inside.

Armed with the hidden camera which we'd hastily repaired, Tony and I simply strolled through the entrance and followed the signs to the maternity ward on the sixth floor. It was the middle of the day but as the lift doors opened, I stepped into a corridor in near darkness. It was eerily quiet, with not a nurse in sight. We decided to split up to look less suspicious.

The only sound was my footsteps; they echoed around the long, narrow corridor. A single beam of sunlight shone through a crack in a boarded window. The now familiar smell of urine lingered in the musty air and strengthened as I passed a door.

As I turned the handle I glanced behind me. If I was discovered I faced certain arrest, but I was still alone in the darkness. The door creaked open and revealed a large, sparse, whitewashed room. A single light bulb flickered above me. It revealed dozens of rows of cots, each one confining a baby or toddler. Their little hands were clinging to the rusting bars that surrounded them, their eyes focused on the empty space above.

Not one was crying; they seemed to be suffering in silence. The first thing they must have learned on these wards is that crying is useless, that nobody comes. They rocked backwards and forwards. It had now become an all too familiar sight, a sign that endless days confined to a cot, without so much as a hug, had left them mentally disturbed. Many of the toddlers couldn't sit up or move their legs, crippled from lying alone without any attention.

In one cot lay a seriously undernourished baby, its little bones visible through papery skin. Lying next to it was another baby with a T-shirt acting as a makeshift nappy, wrapped around the waist and legs.

Tony appeared at the door and told me to follow him. By the entrance to another room full of abandoned toddlers, he had found a baby on the floor wrapped up in a blue blanket. It had a picture of the sacred heart of Jesus pinned to it, along with a note from its mother: 'God look after my child.'

I had rarely seen Tony – a father himself – having to fight so hard to hold back the tears.

What we found in Constanta was just the tip of the iceberg. A British aid worker sneaked us into two other hospitals in Oradea, where she and her friends worked twenty-four hour shifts to try to provide hugs and love to more than eighty abandoned babies kept on the maternity ward. In the nearby children's hospital, where only sick and severely disabled children should be kept, we were shown dozens of perfectly healthy toddlers held in rooms across two floors.

The British aid worker had become good friends with one of the hospital's nurses and persuaded her to be interviewed. We met in our hotel, well away from the hospital. She was a picture of terror as we began to film; although we were hiding her identity, she still feared persecution by the authorities for speaking out.

She began by telling me that nurses like her did care for the children, but they had limited resources: 'Nearly all of the children and babies in our hospitals are abandoned. We try our best but there are too many to look after.' Her eyes started to well up. 'It is heartbreaking to see them suffer. There are just not enough of us to hold them and feed and change them. Sometimes I am the only nurse on the ward.'

And then she confirmed what I already suspected: 'We cannot find any foster parents for them. Babies can be abandoned just because they are ugly or have a birthmark, but most are just unwanted. The hospitals in Romania are like zoos. These babies are trapped in their cots for years and we can see what it is doing to them. They become physically disabled and mentally scarred. We are creating generations of very sick children; they are becoming institutionalised and that makes it even more difficult to persuade foster parents to take care of them. Who wants a child that rocks and cannot talk?'

According to the United Nations Children's Fund UNICEF, around ten thousand babies were being abandoned in Romania every year. The Romanian government fiercely disputed this, admitting only to a figure of five hundred a year.

The nurse was clear on why there was such a discrepancy in the statistics: 'As you know, there are eighty abandoned babies on my ward, but the local Child Protection Service survey states there are just three. This is because we do not have birth certificates or parental release forms for the other seventy-seven. Officially, they do not exist.'

Romania's hospitals were secretly acting as orphanages in a breach of EU law. To make sure we were not witnessing isolated cases, we visited another three hospitals on our journey back to Bucharest and found hundreds of babies lying in silence, trapped in their cots for weeks, months or even years.

Finally, just a mile from the Romanian Parliament in Bucharest, an American aid worker sneaked us into a maternity ward where babies and toddlers had no names, just numbers tied to cots.

'There is nothing wrong with most of them,' the worker said. 'They should be with families.'

From what I now knew, there appeared to be little chance of that happening; for the relatively few seriously disabled children, there was no chance at all. In a side room in the hospital, we found a seven-year-old boy called Ionet. The aid worker told me he had cerebral palsy. His body was stiff and thin; he weighed just twenty pounds and was the size of a one-year-old, fed on a diet of sugared water. He was days from death.

In other beds we found two babies with hydrocephalus, also known as 'water on the brain'. Their heads had expanded to twice the size of their bony bodies. An operation to install a drain for the liquid around their brains would give them a good chance of a normal life, but in their current circumstances that was never going to happen. I stroked their hands and they smiled. It was all I had to offer them.

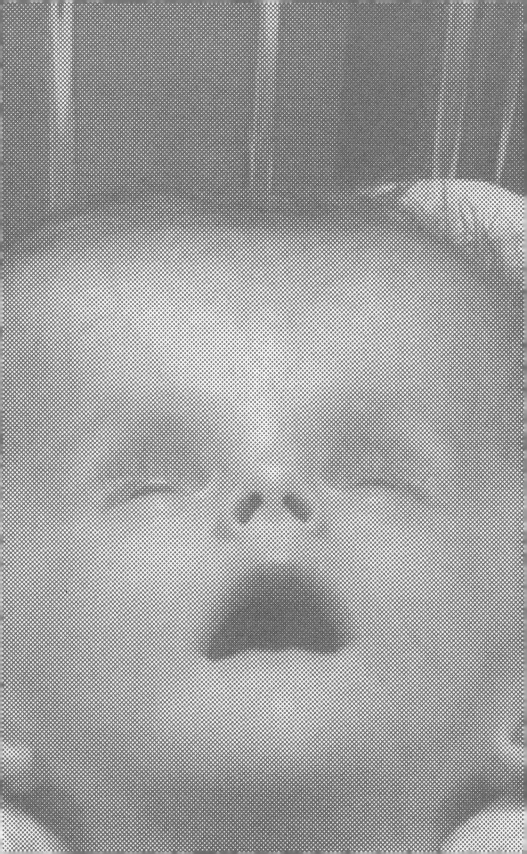

CHAPTER THREE

BABIES FOR SALE

A huge cloud of dust blew around the car as we turned off the main highway onto a dirt track, and in an instant we were transported a hundred years back in time. In the fields, children dressed in rags were playing on bales of straw, getting in the way of farmers who were trying to load the bundles onto horse-drawn carts. We drove over a small stone bridge and, below, a group of women were washing clothes and sheets in a muddy river. All had dark complexions and long black hair. They looked up at us suspiciously; few foreigners were ever seen here.

We were heading into a typical Romanian gypsy village, made up of around forty wooden homes. They were painted brightly in green and blue but, as we got closer, we saw that many of them were no more than shacks in a complete state of disrepair. It was the last stop on our undercover filming trip, and a British aid worker, Sarah Wade, had agreed to bring us here to witness the root causes of some of our most disturbing findings.

Sarah had been fundamental in getting us access to many of the institutions we had visited over the past few days and, after just a short time working together, we had become good friends. Sarah first worked in Romania seven years earlier when she was just nineteen and had remained ever since, unable to tear herself away from the children she came to help. Wise beyond her years, she was also extremely tough. Despite intimidation from the Romanian authorities, she had succeeded in rescuing ten children from a notorious State institution, placing them in her own family-type home, built using funds she had raised herself.

As we turned a tight corner, a horse and cart swerved to avoid us, almost toppling its load of women and children. Sitting in the shade to escape the August sun, other villagers gave us disapproving looks. Tony jumped out of the car excitedly and began to film the picturesque images all around us, a dream assignment for any cameraman.

But while the first impression was of a quaint rural existence, it soon became clear there was also immense poverty. Children played in open sewers outside their makeshift homes, which had neither sanitation nor electricity. As some Romanians embraced their new wealth in the towns and cities, the Roma gypsy community had clearly been left behind.

Sarah told us that many of the abandoned children we had secretly filmed came from villages like this. Hard as it may seem to understand, she explained that many gypsy mothers would rather leave their babies in the care of the State than try to feed another mouth.

Once abandoned to the institutions, the children's sub-human fate was sealed. 'There are about two million Roma gypsies in Romania,' Sarah continued, 'and many Romanians detest them. They are labelled as thieves and beggars, the garbage of the country. That is why the authorities struggle to find foster parents for the abandoned kids. There's a huge shortage of suitable parents, and Romanians rarely want to take home a gypsy or disabled child.'

Sarah was keen for us to meet a family she was trying to help. Her charity had been providing food, clothes and medicine for a single mother called Maria and six of her children.

'It's a mess and so typical of life here. The children all have different fathers. One of them sexually abused his child and was eventually arrested and sent to prison. Maria has left two babies behind in the local maternity hospital; the rest she is determined to keep.'

We found Maria cooking on an open fire at the entrance to her home. She embraced Sarah like an old friend and beckoned us inside with a smile. The shack had just one room for the family of seven, containing a bench and a large, roughly-made wooden bed. Daylight shone through holes in the tiled roof, highlighting piles of rubbish and discarded food everywhere. There was a constant humming from flies, swarming round us and landing in the filth. The conditions were hardly fit for an animal, let alone Maria and her six remaining children.

At first glance Maria looked about forty years old, but Sarah told me she was actually just twenty-five. She had piercing dark eyes but was desperately thin with wrinkled skin, her jet-black hair tangled and matted. We found the youngest of her children, one-year-old David, sleeping on the bed. His face was covered in flies feeding off the food left around his lips. His half-brothers and sisters were outside playing in the open sewer with toy boats made from Coke cans.

Maria immediately began to beg us for money, but we had been warned against handing over any cash: we would almost certainly be cornered as word spread around the village. Instead, Sarah handed her tins of baby milk.

'I know it doesn't look like it,' Sarah commented to us, 'but this woman is really trying to care for her family. We support mothers like her by providing food, milk and clothes, to stop them abandoning their children.'

She acknowledged it was a strategy with limited success. 'Sometimes it works, but a lot of the women just end up selling what we give them at the roadside. We also try to persuade women to use contraception, but they rarely take any notice. They'll have their first child when they're around thirteen – and then have about another ten kids after that.'

Maria took her baby son David in her arms and wiped away the flies crawling around his face. Despite everything I'd heard, I still found what she said next quite shocking. 'I have nothing to offer David, but the nurses and doctors in the hospital will take good care of him – they have food, beds and electricity.'

Sarah desperately tried to explain to Maria that life in institutions was far from what she imagined, but she was having none of it. She had seen the clean rooms and cots in the maternity wards, and that was enough to settle her conscience.

A few days after we left Maria, we heard she had indeed abandoned David in a Romanian hospital. Another gypsy baby had almost certainly just been condemned to years, possibly even his entire life, in grim institutional care.

Sarah told me she strongly believed Romania's ban on international adoption should be lifted to give children like David a better chance of finding a family. As I was about to find out, her view was not only driven by the misery she saw in the local hospitals and institutions: it was also based on personal experience.

She asked me to come to her small flat in Oradea to meet her eight-year-old adopted son, Dylan. She had saved him from a State institution when he was aged one, but it had taken years of wrangling with the authorities and a commitment to live in Romania to complete his adoption.

When we arrived at her modest home, Dylan rushed into Sarah's arms. After a brief introduction, he grabbed my hand and pulled me into his newly-decorated bedroom. It had Spiderman posters and swimming certificates plastered over the walls, and shelves full of teddies and Action Man figures. He dug out some of his favourite toys, shouting: 'Let's play with my Transformers, Chris!'

Meeting Dylan was a shock to the system after endless days witnessing children his age living in absolute misery. I suddenly felt quite emotional, seeing this young boy having fun with his adoptive mother, hugging her, pestering her for attention – all the normal childhood things I had always taken completely for granted back in Britain. Dylan, of course, had no idea just how lucky he was.

'One woman can't save the world, but I can save one child,' said Sarah as she dressed Dylan for bed. 'How can the government say adoption by anyone other than Romanians is not in the best interests of a child – and then send them to stinking institutions where they are confined to a bed day and night, tied up and deprived of love?'

Sarah's experience of the gypsy villages had convinced her it would take a huge shift in culture to tackle the problem, and this was unlikely to happen any time soon. 'Until the government realises that the gypsies need educating and support, abandonment will remain the most popular form of contraception. And in the meantime, international adoption is desperately needed.'

There was another disturbing reason Sarah felt the current situation was unacceptable. Despite the ban, she told us there was a thriving black market in unwanted children. 'Every time I go into a gypsy village, they see I'm a foreigner and the first thing they ask is whether I want to buy their baby.'

Tony and I were stunned. If true, this was a huge story. We had a few days left in Romania and decided we would investigate.

Other aid worker contacts confirmed what Sarah had told us. They'd repeatedly tried to track down missing children, only to find no sign of them in the local hospitals or orphanages. The authorities had no record of their abandonment – they had simply disappeared without trace. Given the large numbers involved, the aid workers were convinced the children were being sold. We were advised to go to one village where several children had vanished in the space of just a few weeks.

The village lay beyond the mountains and Swiss-style chateaux of Transylvania. This stunning part of Romania draws tourists from across the globe. Some come to trace the region's history, steeped in the legend of Count Dracula; others flock to the cheap ski resorts. Could it be that some also come here to buy children on the black market?

Our contacts put us onto a gypsy called Alex, a remarkable character who had left his community to fight in the 1989 Revolution, later becoming an aid worker for a Romanian charity in the hope of improving life back in the gypsy villages where he'd grown up.

Alex had agreed to act as our interpreter and told us to meet him at a crossroads on the outskirts of the village. On first meeting, he appeared completely westernised, sporting a leather jacket and jeans and a slick hair style. He seemed very keen to help us uncover the black market trade, something he said he felt very strongly about.

He told us that the most likely way to buy a child would be to head straight to the elder of the village and tell him what we were looking for. It sounded incredibly risky to me; the elder was effectively the head of the whole community. 'How can we possibly trust him if he is the person in authority?'

'If children were for sale, he would know,' insisted Alex. 'Nothing happens without his knowledge and, if it got to a purchase, he'd be the deal-broker.' He caught my sceptical look and smiled. 'This is Romania, my friend. Everyone is involved in scams like this: the translator and fixer you hire, the elder of the village, the mothers and even the social services. Where do you think the paperwork comes from to get the kids out of the country? All you need is money – and guts, of course.'

It was decision time – we either had to walk away or take Alex's word for it. I reassured myself that, as he'd grown up in these parts, he ought to know the form. But could he be trusted? Was it some kind of trap? We could be arrested, beaten up – or worse.

Safety of journalists in the field is paramount for any news organisation. Throughout the trip we had kept in regular contact with London, often using landlines or email in case our mobiles were being tapped.

As soon as we'd heard about the possible practice of illegally selling children, alarm bells had rung. It was a high-risk story which we hadn't planned for when we came to Romania. From a phone-box outside a remote cafe, I had immediately called the editor of *ITV News*, Deborah

Turness, to tell her about our plans to carry out an investigation. Like me, Deborah was shocked that such a trade could still exist and was keen to proceed, subject to approval from the *ITV News* lawyer and safety officer. Over the years, I have learnt that it's all too easy to get swept along by the pulling power of a great story, allowing your heart to rule your head. But no story is worth losing your life or your freedom for, and the legal and safety experts provide a vital reality check.

A long hour later, Deborah called to give us the verdict: a qualified green light. The lawyer agreed it was in the public interest to investigate. This was crucial as it effectively authorised us to go undercover and film secretly – the only way to expose the trade. The safety officer had the greatest concerns, as we all felt the local police could not be trusted to help us if we got into any kind of trouble. But it was agreed that we knew enough aid workers by now to create a reasonable support team.

The investigation was given a code amber alert, meaning we were to call the newsdesk as we went into the village and call back by a certain time to say we'd left and were safe. We filed exact details of our location, along with phone numbers of local contacts who could help if the newsdesk didn't get that second call. A local lawyer was also placed on standby in case we ended up in jail.

But for all that, only Tony and I could assess the risk on the ground minute by minute as we prepared to enter the village. Both of us had to be happy to proceed, otherwise we pulled the plug. As Tony put on his secret camera rig, he whispered to me: 'Chris, I'm still up for it. For me the importance of exposing this trade outweighs the risks. I think if we don't do it we'll always regret it. What about you?'

Trusting to gut instinct, I nodded my agreement. There was no going back.

The village was different from other gypsy communities we had seen, in that alongside the usual wooden shacks there were a few bungalows, built solidly in stone. And among the horses and carts, I was also surprised to see that some families actually owned cars.

We pulled up outside the largest of the houses. A tall, dark-skinned man approached us. He was quite old, probably in his seventies, and was wearing a tatty brown suit with no shoes. Alex smiled at him, informing us under his breath: 'This is Stefan, the elder of the community. Shall I get straight to it and tell him why you are here?'

Tony and I glanced at each other. 'Go for it, Alex,' I said. 'But give us the nod if you suspect we need to get out of here quick.'

Alex was well-briefed on our cover story. We had decided to pose as two businessmen looking for children to buy to take back to London. Our 'wives' were waiting in a hotel in a nearby town, and if we found children that we wanted, we would supposedly return with our spouses the following day. Only then, so the story went, would we hand over any cash.

The few minutes that it took Alex to relay all this to Stefan seemed like hours, not least as we could follow little of what he was actually saying. I scrutinised the elder's face to see how he was reacting, but it was impossible to be sure. Every now and then he nodded and looked us up and down. To my great relief, as Alex came to an end Stefan smiled and shook our hands.

He led us into the courtyard of his home, circled by a fence made from scraps of metal. There were three toddlers and some older children playing football around us. Stefan beckoned them to a table and began to write messages on scraps of paper. He handed the messages to the children before ushering them out of the yard. In my paranoid state, I was worried he was shopping us to the police, or even summoning a group of locals to come to the yard and beat us up.

'Alex, what is happening?' I asked, trying to appear calmer than I felt. 'He has asked them to deliver messages to women he knows have children for sale. He's instructing them to prepare their homes and clean up their kids, ready to meet you.' The whole atmosphere seemed very relaxed, as if we'd asked Stefan for something routine. Almost immediately, a woman came rushing in to the courtyard and shook his hand, before nodding politely to myself and Tony. I will never forget how cool she was as Alex translated her extraordinary words: 'I am sorry I have no children to offer you. I sold my twins to a Dutch couple last week, but there are many other women here who can help you. We even have an unborn if you want it.'

Her face lit up as she added: 'I used the money to buy sheep and hens. Now I have lots of food and fewer mouths to feed!' On this she burst into laughter and Stefan smiled approvingly.

It was all so shocking and surreal that I struggled to stay in character. Attempting to adopt a businesslike tone, I asked if we could see some of the available children.

The woman nodded enthusiastically. 'We will go and see Nikola. She has done this before and is expecting you.'

We followed Stefan and the woman through a litter-strewn street to Nikola's home, which was cleaner and bigger than most of the others in the village. Nikola, a large and friendly woman, had already lined up her three children. Their demeanour suggested this was not the first time they had been paraded for foreigners.

We were introduced first to Maria, just three years old, with short hair and a dirty face. 'She was named after the Virgin Mary,' explained Nikola. Ella was nine with tangled greasy hair, a torn dress and no shoes. She shook my hand politely, her eyes following me with intense curiosity. Her six-year-old brother, Christian, held out his hand to 'gimme five'. As I slapped his palm, laughter broke out among the crowd around us.

'Who would like to go to London?' Stefan asked. All three children put their hands in the air. 'I already have one daughter in America,' said Nikola. 'The Americans saw her in the hospital where I had abandoned her and came to see me. It was in 1996, before the authorities banned foreigners from taking our children. They offered me cash, enough to buy a new house.'

She was clearly laying out the sort of ball-park figures she was expecting from any negotiation. It also perhaps started to explain some of the stark differences in living conditions we had witnessed in the village.

Nikola continued her bizarre sales patter. 'We were not supposed to accept money for a child so it was like a bribe, I suppose. They seemed good people so I took the money and allowed them to adopt her through the courts – I would never give away a child for free.'

I feigned great interest and asked Stefan how we could buy a child and get it out of the country, given the ban on international adoption. He smiled indulgently, as if amused at the naivety of the question. 'Don't worry, it'll all be sorted out by the local child-protection officer.'

It sounded so unlikely I couldn't hide my surprise. Stefan responded smoothly: 'If you were paid a little to keep the law or a lot to break it, what choice would you make?'

His guard seemed well and truly down as he closed in on what he obviously believed was another lucrative sale. 'In any case, all you need under Romanian law is a letter of consent from the parents to take the child to another country. But we will do better than that. The child-protection people will get you passports for the children, adoption papers and a release form. People will do anything for money here, even at the border. And once you're across, you are in the borderless EU. It's not so difficult, really.'

I glanced at Tony to check he had captured this critical material on the hidden camera. As I expected, he immediately excused himself, asking Alex if he could be directed to a toilet – it was the only safe place to confirm we were filming successfully.

As Tony slipped away, I decided to take a gamble. I asked Nikola if we could use our home video camera to get some footage of her children. 'Our wives would like to come and visit but are a little nervous, so we just wanted to check everything was OK first,' I lied. 'We'd love to get some shots of the children to show them back at the hotel.'

Nikola appeared to buy my spiel and nodded that it was fine. As Tony returned from his toilet break, I handed him the camera. He looked quizzically at me so I reassured him it was 'OK to film a home video.'

Nikola turned to her children and told them to smile for the camera. I handed them chocolate, pretending to choose which one we would like to take home. 'I like Ella and I'm sure my wife will too.'

But to my surprise, Nikola shook her head. 'I am too attached to these ones to give them away, but I have a three-month-old baby in the local hospital who I abandoned because I could not afford her. You can have her.'

After parading the three children so openly, I felt it was simply the opening gambit in a long negotiation. I played along, asking her: 'How much money would we have to pay for your abandoned daughter?'

Nikola lit a cigarette and had an animated conversation with Stefan. Turning to Tony and me, she said: 'I am poor. The Americans gave me enough to buy a new house. My children are worth that kind of money.'

We had no real idea what price she was hinting at, but I had heard rumours of children being bought for around ten thousand pounds. I reckoned an abandoned child would be at the lower end of the 'market' so, in full knowledge that I would never actually be handing over a penny, I offered Nikola five thousand pounds.

It immediately hit the spot. Without hesitation, she leant forward and shook our hands, adding that if it was all right with us, some of the money might have to come in the form of food and clothes so it didn't look too obvious.

To see her reaction, I then decided to up my 'bid' for Ella to eight thousand pounds. Suddenly, the issue was not whether the nine-year-old was up for sale, but how much she was worth. 'I would slit my throat before I sold her for so little,' was Nikola's over-dramatic response. We promised to think things over after we had seen other children.

Stefan escorted us out of the house, smiling and patting my back like I had suddenly become his best friend. 'You will help me build a new roof for my house!' he laughed as he ushered us into another courtyard on the opposite side of the street. Waiting behind the gate was yet another child for sale, a little girl of about five with a sweet smile and stunning blue eyes.

Compared to Nikola's children it looked as if she had been scrubbed up for our meeting. She was wearing a clean, white dress and her hair had been tied in bunches. Her mother picked her up and placed her in my arms. Nobody seemed at all concerned as Tony continued to film on the home video camera.

'Is she for sale?' I asked. 'My wife, in fact both of our wives, would love her. Wouldn't they, Tony?' Tony held the little girl's hand, nodding his 'delight'. Then Stefan began to barter.

'Her name is Andrea. Her mother wants to know if she is going to a good home and, if you take her, will you send letters and photos? If you agree, then she will name a good price. I will also need another one thousand pounds for the social worker to take care of the paperwork.'

By now, nothing I heard surprised me. This black market trade seemed to be a well-oiled machine, involving layer upon layer of corrupt officials. I stroked Andrea's soft face and she smiled at me; it was heartbreaking. Once again I agreed to think things over and see what my 'wife' thought.

Our grotesque shopping trip for children wasn't quite finished. As we left, Stefan cornered me, whispering: 'I have a better child for you to consider, but we must be quick. I do not trust some people here – as word spreads, someone might inform the police for a reward.'

He led us in the direction of the sound of some traditional gypsy music, coming from the window of a small wooden home just round the corner. As we got closer, I could hear clapping and men's voices. Tony slipped the video camera into his bag, leaving just the secret camera rolling – we could not afford to be complacent.

In the back garden, we found a group of men playing homemade instruments and knocking back spirits. We felt very conspicuous as they paused to look us up and down, before returning to their drunken partying.

Behind them stood an elderly woman with a young, pregnant girl at her side. The mother-to-be appeared to be blind in one eye. As we walked towards them, they seemed nervous. Unlike the previous meetings, there was no friendly smile or handshake.

Stefan called them over. 'This is Adena and her mother. Adena is seventeen and is seven months pregnant. They cannot afford another child in this family.'

I nodded and smiled in approval as I imagined a real buyer would. Adena rubbed her swollen stomach, showing no emotion as we examined our prize find. I asked her if she was sad to have to give up a baby.

'No, I cannot give it a good life – there is no room here for another baby. It will be better with you and your wife.'

Tony decided it was as good a moment as any to take out the small video camera and begin filming, but Adena's mother immediately became anxious. I diverted her by asking how much she wanted for her daughter's child.

She responded with an unholy prayer: 'May God bless this child's birth and grant us money in return.' Now I had heard it all.

'When the baby is born, we can talk money,' she concluded, before asking us to leave.

We promised Stefan we would return to the village with our wives the following day. He had no idea, of course, that we would in fact be long gone, heading back to Britain with our explosive footage. Waving goodbye, he was all smiles, like some used-car salesman who had just completed another successful day's business.

As we drove away, I was left trying to make sense of it all. How could any woman, no matter how poor, contemplate selling her child? Nevertheless, as with legal adoption, it was true that some of the children would undoubtedly have a much better quality of life, infinitely so if the alternative was incarceration in one of the appalling institutions we had visited earlier in the trip.

But what if some who came to gypsy villages weren't offering a child a better home? Tony and I could have been traffickers or paedophiles. It was a thought that would haunt me for a long time to come, eventually drawing me back to Romania to report on the abhorrent world of the under-age sex trade.

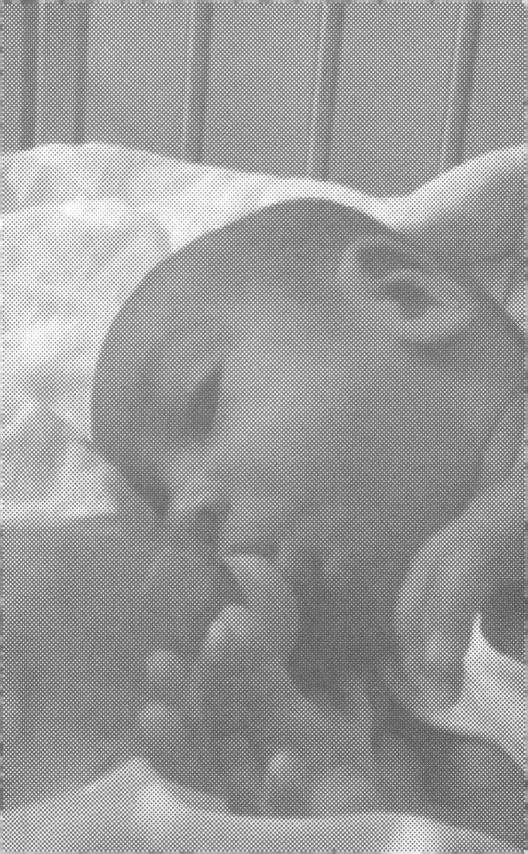

CHAPTER FOUR

THE FALLOUT

September 4th 2006, and standing by the fax machine in the newsroom, I had rarely been more nervous. In just a few hours' time, the shocking images we had secretly filmed in Romania's orphanages would be broadcast on the *ITV Evening News* in the UK, on *NBC News* in America and across the world on CNN. It was a massive story for ITV which we knew would create global shock-waves.

I had sent a detailed description of our findings to the Romanian government, and their official response was due to be faxed over at any minute. Every line of my script and every frame of the footage had been checked by our lawyer and independent medical experts, but however sure of my facts, it was a sobering thought that I was about to go on air accusing a fellow European country of appalling negligence. Knowing their track record of intimidation and cover-ups, I was not expecting the Romanian leadership to take it lying down.

A few weeks earlier during my research, I had received the chilling personal threat from a Romanian official who warned me not to attempt to expose any cruelty in the country's institutions. And throughout my undercover journey across Romania, I had met many aid workers who feared for both their safety and the future of their charity work because they had agreed to help me.

At the very least, I anticipated a robust denial from the Romanian government, followed by a smear campaign to discredit my journalism. As the fax machine kicked into life, I took a deep breath. The *ITV News* lawyer and the news editor Deborah Turness joined me to read their reaction. Defending the indefensible is an art perfected by many a government publicity machine, but the statement issued by Bogdan Paniat, the Romanian minister for Child Welfare, plumbed breathtaking new depths. Scanning the fax, I found it hard to take in the words.

The *ITV News* reports are a propaganda war that has nothing to do with Romanian children, or the respect of human rights in Romania. It is a cheap attempt to attract the attention of viewers during the quiet holiday period, as if the old stereotype about Romanian children was more interesting for the public than other events taking place worldwide.

We believe Mr Rogers and ITN (*ITV News*) have used old images from twenty years ago and hired actors for their investigation, in a cheap attempt to discredit Romania's forthcoming membership of the European Union.

If indeed there are children whose families agreed to sell them for USD 10,000, we will investigate and we will punish the culprits, either the parents or the local authorities.

Romanian legislation forbids the institutionalisation of children under 3 years old, because Romanians recognised the negative effects on a baby's development if he or she is placed in an institution. Only in the cases of children with disabilities, which need specialised care, the placement in a residential institution is permitted.

We are aware that it is time to deal increasingly
with the quality of care given to children in the
new types of institutions — homes, apartments,
and small centres.

We also know that priority must be given to
training the staff directly responsible with the
care of children.

The first few sentences drew gasps and snorts of derision from many in the newsroom. The ludicrous accusations smacked of complete desperation by a government that had no genuine defence, and I was confident they would instantly be seen as such by the European Union.

While the statement blatantly ignored our findings – and was clearly libellous – the ITV lawyer nevertheless felt it contained a crucial admission that Romania still had some way to go to improve its child welfare. This was highly significant, as a decent standard of care for the country's children was a condition set by the EU for membership.

More reaction came through on the fax, this time from Theodora Bertzi, Romania's Secretary of State for Adoptions. Unlike her government colleague, she didn't actually accuse us of fabricating our reports, but instead ducked the issue by insisting we had highlighted only rare, isolated cases of lack of care.

The newsroom fell silent as the evening news went live, and as the now familiar images played out on all the monitors, some producers quietly left the room in tears. I had been so involved in getting the story on air that I had momentarily forgotten the true horror of what we had found.

The reaction in the UK to the broadcast was phenomenal. The *ITV News* switchboard went into meltdown, and within a few minutes I had received more than a hundred emails from British viewers expressing their shock at what they had seen.

A short time later, many in Romania were also witnessing the distressing images on CNN International. Senior *ITV News* executives joined me to monitor how the story was being handled by Romanian State Television, which was being fed into the newsroom via a satellite feed. The channel was broadcasting what it described as a 'special news programme' to discuss my reports.

At first, it seemed the programme was simply reflecting the shocking findings, with the presenter introducing clips from my investigations into the treatment of children in institutions and their sale in gypsy villages. But then he handed over to a reporter, who was apparently broadcasting live from an institution. The room he was standing in looked clean, with pictures of Disney characters on the wall, and he was surrounded by happy, well-dressed children.

'This is one of the institutions Chris Rogers visited,' the reporter stated, but if it was, I certainly didn't recognise it.

'As you can see it is very clean and the children are happy here. None of them are tied up as he claimed. It is highly unlikely he filmed those images here recently.'

It was gobsmackingly crude. Would the Romanian people really buy this propaganda? The presenter crossed over to another supposed reporter in a gypsy village. Standing beside him were two mothers holding their children lovingly in their arms.

By now a crowd of colleagues had gathered around the television set to watch the Romanian 'news' programme, and there was a roar of laughter as the reporter asked the women if they would ever consider selling their children – as if they would admit such a thing on national television.

The response was not exactly a surprise: 'No, we love our children; we would never give them away.'

The programme grew ever more surreal to watch, culminating in a studio interview with the Romanian minister Bogdan Paniat, allowing him to peddle unchallenged his fantastic yarn about how we'd fabricated our reports.

'What is your reaction to the claims of ITV, Mr Paniat?' asked the presenter solemnly.

'Well, I have not watched the reports in full, but it is my belief that they are old images from twenty years ago. We were warned that western journalists will target Romania in the run-up to our membership of the European Union.'

The following night, *ITV News* broadcast my second investigation, focussing on the sale of Romanian children, and we also decided to show clips of the way Romanian State TV had treated the story. By now, we were experiencing one of the largest viewer responses in the history of *ITV News*. Some viewers called the switchboard weeping, others emailed or called to say they were so deeply moved that they wanted to help in any way they could. Later I was to find out that one of the viewers moved to action was none other than the Duchess of York.

Although both reports had now been seen across the globe, we had heard nothing from the European Union. So I was told to grab my passport, pack my bags and head to the EU Parliament building in Strasbourg to deliver our evidence and report on their reaction.

I requested a meeting with Olli Rehn, the Commissioner responsible for the expansion of the EU and the man who had championed Romania's accession, but he refused to see me. The aim was to file a report on the EU position for that day's evening news, and with just an hour to go before we were due to go on air, I finally managed to track down the Commissioner. As he left the debating chamber, I forced a copy of my investigations into his hand. My cameraman filmed him trying to get away from me, looking embarrassed. He would not give any comment, instead promising a response in the coming days.

I found it hard to understand how the EU could be so slow off the mark to react to such a major story. It only served to give the impression they had something to hide. I ran back to our hotel and quickly put together a news piece on the lack of reaction, feeding it back just in time to get on air.

The scandal of Romania's orphanages gathered momentum, with many newspapers picking up on the story and celebrities and politicians calling for a change in Romania's adoption policy. A growing number of MEPs – Members of the European Parliament – demanded an urgent review of Romania's fitness to join the European Union.

Olli Rehn wrote to the MEPs, making it clear he was in no doubt more could be achieved if Romania's membership went ahead:

In respect of recent television reports on child protection problems in Romania, I am aware that Romania and indeed other European countries have some way to go in reforming institutional care. The EU has a choice, close the doors and punish or keep them open and help. I personally believe Romania has come a long way in respect of child protection, and it has shown its commitment to child welfare in accordance with conditions set for accession.

But the pressure continued to mount, and by the end of the week there was a dramatic announcement by the EU Monitoring Committee responsible for Romania. In reaction to my investigation, criteria for the country's membership and its ban on international adoption would be reviewed during a debate in Brussels. It was to be held just two months before Romania was due to join the European club at the start of 2007.

The guest list for the debate included not only MEPs and commissioners but members of the Romanian government, including Bogdan Paniat and Theodora Bertzi. Also invited to speak were some of the world's leading experts in child care, psychology and institutionalisation – and myself.

To have been so influential in triggering the debate was a great coup for *ITV News*, but it gave us the intriguing problem of how best to communicate its significance to the audience. The minutiae of European Parliament business rarely set the world on fire, even when they involve such an emotive subject. In discussion with my editor Deborah, we agreed that the answer was to try to find a further story in Romania, which would highlight the issues surrounding adoption of children by foreigners.

Deborah was naturally concerned that returning to Romania might put me in too much danger. I was a marked man, not exactly popular with the Romanian authorities. Even if I got through passport control, operating in the country would be extremely difficult.

But having come so far, I was happy to give it a go. I knew that other journalists who'd criticised Romania had managed to slip back into the country, so I suspected the border controls weren't particularly thorough. There was still the possibility I would be arrested and deported but, having thrashed out the risks with the lawyer and the safety officer, my return trip was given the go-ahead. However, we had to proceed with the usual 'code amber' precautions in place – much as we had for our undercover visit to the gypsy village to report on the sale of children.

That still left the almost insuperable problem of finding a story I could actually film. As feared, nearly all of the aid workers who had cooperated with me had been kicked out of the country. Sarah Wade and a few others had avoided expulsion, but they'd been summoned to Bucharest by the Child Protection Services to be told their charity projects and licences to operate in Romania were now under review.

It was heart-rending to find that the very people who had helped me were being persecuted by the authorities. Even more disturbing was that many of the children we had filmed were now being denied the essential care provided by the charity workers. The draconian action against British and American aid workers made headlines on both sides of the Pond. *USA Today* put it bluntly: 'Romanian Child Abuse: American and Brit charity workers expelled in cover-up.'

Under the headline 'Barred: The aid workers who exposed Romania's orphan abuse', the *Mail on Sunday* reflected the general dismay that a supposedly civilised government could be so heartless as to take action which made conditions even worse for vulnerable children:

```
A young woman, who had been working in an
institution in the north of Romania and wished
to remain anonymous, said: 'I knew this would
happen. The images are everywhere but they live
in denial.'

Six staff from the UK charity The Smiles
Foundation working in the same institution have
also been told to go.

The charity said last night: 'The State hospitals
are stretched in their resources and charitable
organisations have been caring for abandoned,
abused and neglected children to tremendous
effect. Now we have been told to leave.'
```

With nobody left to help me on the ground, I turned for inspiration to the hundreds of emails from viewers. Many expressed their disgust and anguish, as they had truly believed Romania had sorted out its problems. As I worked through my inbox, there were offers of help from top surgeons and doctors, students and housewives. Viewers from America to Australia wanted addresses of charities so they could send donations. A group of mothers in London had staged fund-raising events, while a school in Scotland was planning a jumble sale to raise money.

The celebrity world also muscled in. Supermodel and actress Lisa B proposed a trip to Romania with me – while not quite what I was looking for at that moment, it would later inspire a high profile campaign, in which she would use famous mothers to highlight the mistreatment of children.

Nestling among the endless extraordinary messages, I came across a story which I instantly felt could be perfect to mark the EU debate. The email was not from a rich donor, politician or celebrity, but an unknown British woman called Beverly Peberdy.

```
Dear Chris,


I watched your reports on ITV News and I am
devastated to see such poor children in horrific
conditions but I am not surprised. I have seen it
first hand too, although it was many years ago.
While like many people, I believed improvements
had been made to orphanages in Romania, it does
not surprise me that the suffering still goes
on. Unfortunately, those unwanted souls will
never be the priority of a country with so many
other problems to fix. Besides a few 'showcase'
orphanages, it is depressing that conditions
in most homes have barely changed since I was
```

there in the early nineties. In 1991, after the
fall of communism in Romania, I like millions of
others was horrified by the television pictures of
orphanages in Romania. I felt compelled to quit
my job in a building society and go out there to
work as a charity volunteer. I was sent to an
orphanage called Ungerini, east of the city of
Bacau. I adopted an abandoned child from there
and brought him up in the UK. He was a 3 year old
boy called Patreascu who'd had polio, and I found
him in a room where sick babies were left to die.
Patreascu is now a healthy 19 year old and wants
to learn about his past by returning to the place
where he spent the hellish first few years of his
life. I thought this may be of interest to you.
My husband John and I are most proud of the fact
that he has, of his own free will, decided to
return to Romania to investigate his past, in the
hope he can make a difference for those who were
left behind. Perhaps you could film his trip to
Romania? Patreascu and I feel strongly that many
of the children in your reports could have been
saved by foreigners who would be more willing
than Romanians to adopt them.

I couldn't believe my luck – if we could pull it off, this remarkable story
would be an extremely powerful complement to the European Union
debate on international adoption. I immediately got in touch with
Beverley and Patreascu and began planning to film his personal journey
back to the orphanage he'd been rescued from all those years ago.

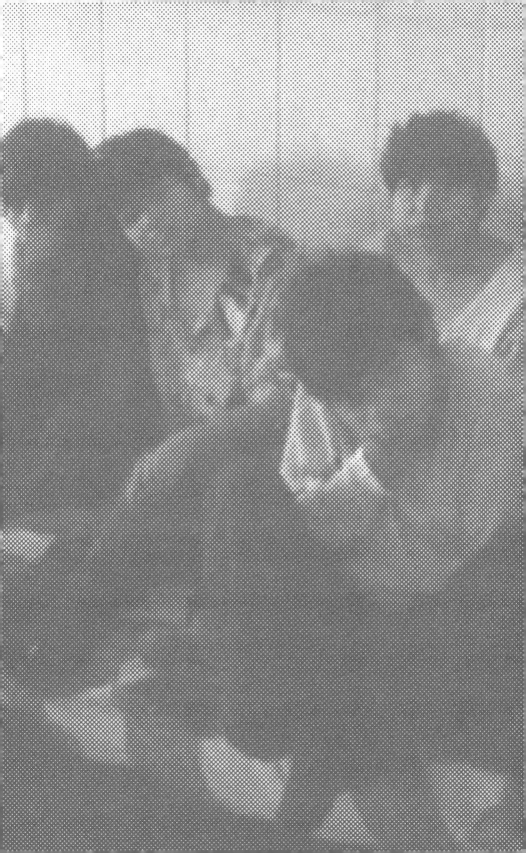

CHAPTER FIVE

PATREASCU'S STORY

Patreascu and I agreed that we should not to travel to Romania together. My potential arrest could scupper the entire trip if we were caught by the authorities, and the last thing I wanted was to jeopardise his return to the orphanage.

I also needed to interview his adoptive parents Beverly and John without his presence, so as Patreascu went ahead into Romania, my cameraman and I diverted to the holiday island of Cyprus, where they had recently moved to spend their retirement. It was to be a one-day pit-stop at their villa in the hills, just outside a bustling tourist resort.

Beverly greeted me at the door with a hug and a glass of home-made lemonade. She struck me as very motherly, a larger-than-life character with long curly hair, rosy cheeks and a constant smile. Her husband John was lying in the garden, looking like a typical Brit abroad: a big fellow with a round suntanned face and grey, thinning hair. We sat on the porch admiring the stunning views of the ocean, which reflected the bright yellows and reds of the sunset. It was the perfect setting for the interview.

As the cameraman finished setting up, Beverly opened a tin box full of photos of Patreascu. She proudly pulled out a bundle and showed me pictures of his sixth birthday party, the first at his new home in the UK. There were photos documenting every stage of his recovery in British hospitals, from near-death to a healthy, energetic child. 'We never planned to adopt a child, you know. We were happy with our life and our son Russell. But events just snowballed.'

John hardly got a word in as Beverly chatted away, taking me through Patreascu's typical British childhood and explaining how he'd quickly become a high-achieving pupil, winning a scholarship to attend a private school in Milton Keynes. Dozens of other photos followed, showing Patreascu scuba-diving, jet-skiing, horse-riding, and generally being involved in just about any activity going.

They were like any proud parents, but I couldn't help thinking just how special all this was – when they first found Patreascu in Romania, he had been left for dead. As if on cue, John pulled out a tatty black and white photo from the bottom of the tin and passed it to me, stating sombrely: 'It is unlikely that any of the other children from the orphanage survived.'

It was an image I had now become familiar with, naked children with skeletal bodies, some with their hands tied to the bars of their cots. John continued, his voice cracking with emotion: 'If they did survive then they will be in a terrible state, I am sure. Going by your investigation, very little has changed in those appalling institutions. We couldn't save them all, Chris.'

Beverly handed me another photo of Ungerini's children. 'These are the kids we found there all those years ago.' Her eyes began to well up. 'It's important Patreascu knows it was just luck that we chose him and not any of the other 185 children. We had to leave them behind in the orphanage; we could only take one home. In a strange kind of way Patreascu chose us, we didn't choose him – and only someone who has adopted a child will understand what I mean by that.'

Beverly pulled out more photos of emaciated children in rusting cots. I had been about to ask her about her time as a volunteer in the orphanage, but her compelling story poured out unprompted.

'It was like working in a madhouse. I couldn't imagine that hell could be any more frightening a place.' She recalled everything as though it had happened just days ago. It was clearly a hugely significant time in her life.

'I remember my first day. It was cold and there had been a heavy snowfall. The charity bus pulled up outside the gates of the orphanage to drop me off with five other volunteers. An unshaven security guard stumbled out, wrapped in sheepskin to keep warm. He fumbled for ages, struggling with the rusting padlock. Eventually he pulled the gates open and we walked through the forbidding entrance in the slush, passing under the wrought-iron sign bearing the name of the home which housed hundreds of unwanted children: Ungerini Irrecuperable Hospital.

'It looked more like a factory, a grey concrete building with a huge chimney, smoke billowing out of the top. But then I spotted the tiny faces of children pressed against the barred windows, trying to see who it was that had come to visit. As I walked through the door I didn't feel any escape from the cold: there was no heating. Water dripped from the ceilings and down the crumbling walls. It took quite some time to adjust my eyes to the darkness of the corridors, and only then did I see the pitiful little scraps rocking manically and moaning. Others were still and silent, tied by their hands and feet to their cots. There was no interaction, nothing for them to do. It was as if they were just lying there waiting to die.'

Beverly was told to work in what had become known as 'the dying room', where very sick toddlers and children were condemned to spend their final days.

'I fed my little sick patients with a milk powder mixture and sugared water which I placed on their tongues with a syringe. Food and medicine were scarce.'

She handed me another photo of two almost naked toddlers lying in the same cot, their legs bent back and tied with straps of material. They looked painfully thin and dirty.

'The one on the right is Patreascu and the other is a little boy called Iulien. They were the sickest children in the dying room. We took these photos so I could show people back home just how bad things were – little did I know then that one of those boys would become my son.

'Patreascu was so poorly. He was suffering from severe bronchial trouble, which I later learnt was an after-effect of polio. He was tied up to stop him escaping from his cot – though he couldn't even sit up or crawl, let alone walk. Iulien was suffering from malnutrition and chronic ear infections, and both of them showed signs of institutionalisation. I was determined to save them and called on John to send out some medical supplies from the UK. Iulien made a steady recovery, but the condition of many of the other children got worse, and the sickest of them all was Patreascu.

'I was desperate for some kind of miracle, and just when I was about to give up hope, it came. Mother Teresa's Order, Missionaries of Charity, had built a care home nearby and told us they had room to take a few of our most vulnerable and dying children. They suggested we select three children from each room. It was the hardest decision I have ever had to make in my life. In the end, I persuaded them to take eight children from the dying room, including of course Patreascu. For the other dear ones left behind, I have never got over the feeling that I betrayed them and left them to end their days in misery.'

At this critical moment in the story, we had to pause to do a tape-change, which meant we had already filmed half an hour's worth of material. It was all vital background for my report on Patreascu's return to Ungerini, but I also felt deeply moved to be hearing firsthand such an extraordinary tale. Having recently witnessed similar awful scenes myself, but being unable to intervene while filming undercover, I found Patreascu's story a powerful symbol of hope.

With the camera rolling again, Beverly picked up from where she'd left off: 'It was remarkable what a bit a food, warmth and love from the Sisters did for him. But Patreascu also needed special surgery as the polio had badly affected one leg. It was six inches shorter than the other, which had also withered through having been tied, knees to chest, for so many years.'

The Sisters suggested to Beverly that she took Patreascu to Britain for emergency surgery and therapy. 'It all seemed such a natural move to make. Only now looking back do I realise what a huge task I had agreed to. Patreascu underwent an immensely complicated operation to extend his leg. Over the next nine months, his leg was lengthened by six inches, using innovative equipment inserted during surgery.

'During this time, we took him regularly back to our home, where he became part of the family. We had to teach him to walk using stabilisers, and he was still suffering from the emotional effects of institutionalisation. At times he completely withdrew from the world around him. He couldn't talk because no one had taught him to. What he needed was something he had never experienced: a normal childhood. As we gave him that, not only did he make a remarkable recovery but we developed an inevitable, unbreakable bond. How could we ever let him go back to Romania?'

Their story took another unexpected turn as Beverly went on to explain the part played by Mother Teresa, the world-renowned head of Missionaries of Charity, based in Calcutta in India. 'If it wasn't for her, we would not have been able to adopt Patreascu. On the night we decided we wanted him to stay with us in the UK, I called Sister Jane, Superior at the Convent in Bacau and asked her if she thought it was a good idea. I remember being quite astonished by her reply – she said she had always had him designated for us but was waiting for both of us to want him.'

'I was even more surprised when she told me that we had to contact Mother Teresa herself to obtain official permission to begin the adoption process. She gave me a number in Calcutta, and when I called it, a soft but strong voice answered the phone – it was her. I told her about our fight for Patreascu's life and how we could not bear the thought of sending him back. She sounded so warm and excited for us and immediately gave us her blessing – but making me promise to do everything legally. I will always remember her parting words: "God bless you, your husband, Russell and Patreascu."'

It took Beverly and John a total of three exhausting years to fight through the bureaucracy before the adoption was finalised. While the seemingly endless process ground on, they decided it was important for Patreascu's birth parents to know about their plans, even though his parents hadn't seen him since shortly after his birth.

'All the time I had been at Ungerini, I found it shocking that the parents were willing to just dump their children in institutions and forget about them. I wanted to meet his family to at least understand why they left him. And in a maternal way, I wanted them to know he was in safe hands.'

The Sisters traced Patreascu's family to a small farming community in a mountainous region far from Bacau. With no way to contact the family, Beverly and John took the nerve-racking decision to turn up unannounced.

'They were all desperately poor, no shoes on their feet and a shack for a home. His mother Elena was blonde, which surprised me since Patreascu was so dark. She was an attractive woman with troubled green eyes. The family had already heard we were planning to adopt their son, and told me they were ashamed to meet me because they could imagine what we thought of them for abandoning Patreascu on the first day of his life.

'But they said they had genuinely believed they were sending him to a place where he would be better looked after, and Elena insisted that every day since his birth she had thought about him. His grandfather revealed that he once made the journey to see Patreascu, but seeing how handicapped he was, had decided, with sadness, that it would be impossible for them to look after him.

'I promised the family that, when the time was right, I would explain everything to Patreascu, and said that one day I was sure he would want to visit them. They seemed comforted by this, and Elena grabbed some photographs of herself and Patreascu's father and handed them to me. I was moved to tears and humbled as she kissed my hands, thanking me for taking care of her son.'

Beverly paused to give me an envelope. I was quite overwhelmed when she told me what was inside: 'This contains those photos of Patreascu's parents. I have also slipped in a note with the name of the village where they live. Patreascu has so far rejected any suggestion that he should go and visit them. But just in case he changes his mind, you can hand him this.'

Instead of being an impartial observer, I suddenly felt a great responsibility to all the different parties involved in this deeply personal human drama.

In the coming days the next act would play out as Patreascu fulfilled his wish to return to the place where he was left to die. If the institutions I had visited just a few weeks earlier were anything to go by, he was about to see a disturbing vision of what might have been.

*

My cameraman and I decided to split up as we headed to passport control at Bucharest airport; at least that way he would still get in if I didn't. I had already discussed a 'Plan B' to sneak back into the country over one of its remote borders, should I fail to get past Customs. Rightly or wrongly, I was far more worried about failing to film the story than my personal safety.

I tried to look relaxed and smiled a 'Hello' as I handed my passport to the guard. Even if Romanians didn't know my face, they would certainly know my name, which had been splashed across newspapers and TV for days. But to my huge relief, the guard didn't even take my passport from my hand, simply waving me through as a welcome European Union citizen. Ironically, it seemed border controls were already relaxing in anticipation of the impending EU membership.

I felt quite smug as we drove through the congested streets of Bucharest towards the motorway that would take us north. I was travelling freely in a country where I was probably the government's public enemy number one.

It was a two hundred mile drive to Bacau, situated in the historic region of Moldovia in the foothills of the Carpathian Mountains. The city is a mixture of stunning Moldovian architecture and monstrous concrete disasters erected by the communists, our hotel unfortunately being one of the latter. As we walked in, a voice yelled across the lobby: 'Welcome to Romania!' It was Patreascu, looking like a typical grungy, westernised student, with long hair and round glasses. Only his tanned skin and dark hair hinted at his Romanian heritage.

We decided to get to know each other over a few beers and a game of pool in the bar. As we walked over, I quickly noticed he still bore the scars of his childhood, with a marked limp and slightly unclear speech at times. He was keen to learn more about television, telling me that he was already working as a cameraman at a local TV station in Cyprus.

I steered the subject round to his return to Romania, and was surprised at his reaction to setting foot in the country of his birth after so long. He claimed to be unimpressed, finding it quite 'grim' and 'typical Eastern Bloc'. When I quizzed him about his early childhood, he seemed keen to avoid the subject, even ignoring me at times. I was intrigued and asked him directly: 'Why don't you want to talk about what happened to you here?'

He seemed a little agitated. 'Look, I don't remember anything about my life here. I know what happened because I was told by my adoptive parents – my mum and dad as far as I'm concerned – but I never talk about my past. It's easier to ignore the fact you were rejected at birth and dumped in an institution than it is to face up to it.'

It was an understandable reaction to what he'd been through, but it didn't quite square with the fact that he had invited me to film his journey back to the orphanage. Apart from my personal concern about how I was going to get any sound bites for my report, I was also worried that, deep down, he might not be ready to retrace his steps.

'I know I don't want to visit my birth parents. Why should I?' he responded. 'I have been told time and time again that they did care about me but how could they? Even so, I do want to go to Ungerini because I know how important this film could be. I want to help those left behind and I don't want to let anyone down.'

*

Like most orphanages in Romania, Ungerini was in a remote area well away from the cities – perhaps so people could easily forget the unwanted inmates housed there. The grey building was just as grim and industrial as Beverly had described it. As we passed through the gates, I spotted hands banging against the barred windows, just as they did when she first arrived in 1991. Could it really be that little had improved in over fifteen years?

One thing had clearly got worse: the staff at Ungerini were particularly unwelcoming to foreign visitors. A young, sour-faced woman dressed in medical whites came running out of the entrance, gesturing for us to turn around and leave. Our interpreter jumped out of the car and explained that we were expected, but unfortunately it didn't quite do the trick.

'Only Mr Patreascu can come inside – he is Romanian but no foreign visitors!' she shouted in English. 'They are not allowed now because they could be journalists. No cameras and only Romanians.'

I smiled ruefully: this would have been a direct order to all institutions following my investigations. My cameraman grabbed his bag and pulled out his phone, stills camera and a small home video camera, shouting to the nurse: 'We will leave all this in the car; we will not film. We are just friends of Patreascu.' His quick thinking paid off and wearily she beckoned us inside. As ever, we'd taken the precaution of rigging hidden cameras to document everything we found.

It was the first time I had entered an orphanage and not been hit by the stench of urine and body odour. Instead, there was a strong smell of chlorine. The floors of the corridor and the white tiles on the walls were gleaming, and there were endless displays of children's posters pinned to cork-boards.

The very nature of investigative journalism means you often have little idea of what you will come across. It quickly flashed through my mind that in this case the story might be Patreascu witnessing a much-improved system for the children that were still there. EU funds had certainly reached some State institutions – though usually the ones that the authorities showed off openly to the world. With the nurse so reluctant to let us in, I remained open-minded.

We followed her along the corridor to a door which she unlocked. She asked us to wait as she slipped through, relocking the door behind her. It was clear she was checking all was in order for our tour. Through the door I could hear the clanking of metal buckets and people rushing around, along with the screams and moans of the mentally ill.

The door eventually creaked open and, as the nurse ushered us through, I could see other staff putting away mops and buckets. The smell of disinfectant was overpowering. To my great surprise, I realised that the noise was coming not from children but adults.

There were around twenty men and women sitting on two large wooden platforms covered with rugs. They were all dressed in rags soiled by food or soaked in urine; many had shaved heads. It was the Romania I had seen so many times now, a living hell for the sick and unwanted. I glanced at Patreascu: he looked like he was in shock.

'Are you ok?' I asked. 'Just try to go with the flow.'

But he remained uncharacteristically quiet. I would later learn he was suffering horrific flashbacks to his early childhood, terrible memories he had been able to suppress until now.

The room was sparse and clinical, covered in white tiles from floor to ceiling. There was no television or radio, not even chairs to sit on or cupboards for personal belongings. So with absolutely nothing to stimulate them, the residents resorted to rocking back and forth. Every single one of them did it, some violently. They didn't even notice they had visitors.

I had, sadly, seen this behaviour many times before; it was a classic sign of boredom and distress. One young man covered his head with his hooded jumper, placed his hands over his dirty face and screamed as he rocked. In the far corner of the room another teenager grabbed his ears with his hands and persistently smashed the back of his head against the tiled wall. You could hear the thud reverberate through his skull with every impact. I couldn't bear it any longer and did the natural thing, reaching over to try to stop him before he cracked his head open. But he screamed and cowered as if I were going to hit him. The nurse just stood impassively in the centre of the room. Then she looked at her watch as if to suggest our brief visit was over.

'Where are the children?' Patreascu asked her.

'There are no children here; we have one hundred and twenty young adults in these rooms,' she replied, in a matter of fact tone. 'When we became full we stopped taking any more children, and Ungerini was later reclassified as an adult institute.'

The awful truth dawned on Patreascu that he was face-to-face with what would almost certainly have been his own destiny. 'Oh my God!' he exclaimed. 'They've been here all their lives. No wonder they appear so disturbed. There's nothing for them to do here.'

His outburst did not go down well with the nurse. 'OK, you have seen what you wanted to see. It is time for you and your friends to go.' But having come so far, Patreascu was not budging. There was still a crucial missing piece of his personal jigsaw puzzle. 'I shared a cot with a boy called Iulien Boanta. I would like to know if he is still here.'

'Iulien … Iulien … ' the nurse mumbled, shaking her head to indicate she couldn't recall the name. 'Now, it really is time to go,' she demanded.

'But if these people have been here all their lives, then Iulien must be here,' Patreascu insisted angrily.

The nurse shrugged her shoulders. 'We can have a look at the record books, if it is so important for you to know.'

As we made our way to the office, she talked more about the conditions: 'We have had double-glazing and heating installed and the entire building has been refurbished, but as you can see we still need more furniture, and we need equipment to provide therapy. They just clean these places up and leave us to it. We try our best.'

Although some things had clearly improved since Beverly was last here, it was, as the nurse acknowledged, still a God-forsaken existence for the inmates – even worse in many ways, as they had endured it for so long and there was no hope of a better life.

The nurse led us into a smoky office and threw a pile of books onto her desk. 'If Iulien is still here, you will find his name in these records. You can look for your entry too.'

Patreascu started down the listings, each one showing name, date of birth, date of arrival at the institute and family address where known. Many entries had red lines drawn through them.

Anticipating our question, the nurse explained: 'A red line means they have died. A black one means that, like you, they left Ungerini, perhaps with a foster or adoptive family.' Patreascu flicked through page after page in silence, before practically leaping out of his chair in excitement. 'I found it! There I am!'

The entry had a clear black line through it. His finger rested on the names of his parents. 'My God, there is the name of my Romanian family – but no address.'

Patreascu's elation at finding his name quickly changed into what appeared to be anger. 'I don't want to see them anyway. What am I going to say to them – thanks for dumping me in this hell-hole? Thanks for leaving me to spend day after day rocking on a bed with twenty others?'

I had actually brought to the orphanage the envelope containing Patreascu's parents' photos and whereabouts, but if it was ever going to be handed over to him, now was clearly not the right time. Patreascu turned back to the record book to continue the search.

'Iulien, Iulien, Iulien, Iulien Boanta ... he must be here somewhere.' He flicked through more pages, then another book and another, becoming increasingly desperate. Suddenly, his index finger stopped halfway down a page and he exclaimed: 'He's dead! He's dead!'

Iulien's entry had a red line drawn right through it. The nurse sighed deeply – it was clearly not a surprise to her. 'Most do not live past twenty. It is the drugs, you see.'

Patreascu was silent; we all were. We probably should have guessed that this was a likely outcome, but strangely none of us had expected the awful news. The nurse picked up the phone: 'I am calling the local social worker. She will know what happened to your friend.'

She launched into a conversation in Romanian, scribbling away on a notepad, before turning back to us. 'OK. In 2004, Iulien became very ill and was sent to a new institution in Bacau. The facilities are good there and it was hoped he would get better, but he died a few weeks later from liver failure. This is very common because in Romania we give patients alcohol-based drugs to calm them down – it numbs their troubled minds.'

Clearly distraught, Patreascu got up to leave. The nurse ripped a page from her notebook, grabbed him and stuffed the crumpled paper in his hand. 'This is the address of the cemetery where he's buried. You will find his grave there.'

*

Patreascu slumped into the back seat of the car, saying little as we left Ungerini. The last time he passed through these gates and into the outside world, he was too young to know how lucky he was. This time, in the most awful circumstances, he could not have been more aware.

We had travelled for less than a mile when everything suddenly seemed to hit him, and he became extremely agitated and emotional. I desperately wanted to find the words to comfort him, but at that moment there was little anyone could say. He asked us to pull over, saying he wanted to be on his own and take a walk.

By chance, we had stopped on a hillside with a clear view back across the valley to the orphanage. As Patreascu walked along the country lane, we took the opportunity to pull out our large camera with its long lens to get some exterior shots of Ungerini. It would later prove to have been a very careless thing to do.

Patreascu returned to the car a little calmer, saying that he was keen to see Iulien's grave. I felt he had probably had enough trauma for one day, but in the end it was his call. The atmosphere was subdued as we made our way to the city cemetery.

Amid all the emotion, I had to remember I was here to do a job, even though at times like this it felt quite intrusive. It was important to try to interview Patreascu to get his true feelings on camera while they were still raw. To my relief, he was keen to get some of his thoughts out of his system.

'Being there again brought back memories of the suffering. Not vivid memories but more like emotions I knew I had felt before: feelings of rejection and being so sick. It freaked me out. I looked at their faces and kept thinking how lucky I was to escape. The whole situation is so sad but it also made me angry, because if fate had played things differently I could still be there as one of them – or more likely dead.'

The cemetery was the largest in Bacau, an immense mass of marble pillars, tombs and headstones. We had no idea where to begin to look for Iulien's grave. Our interpreter asked a gardener where we were most likely to find the burial place of children from Ungerini and he directed us to the very far end of the grounds. As we got closer, the air filled with the stench of rubbish and rotting food. We could hear bulldozers and scavenging birds.

On a hill right next to the city rubbish dump, we found a cluster of simple wooden crosses, the graveyard for Ungerini's dead. It appeared the patients were neglected in death just as they had been in their short lives. The names inscribed on each cross had almost weathered away, and many of the crosses were lying on their sides in the overgrown grass.

With tears in his eyes, Patreascu lifted a fallen cross and stamped it upright into the ground, revealing the faded name of the boy he had come to find, Iulien Boanta. 'We are probably the only ones who've ever come to visit him,' he said. 'Poor Iulien. Maybe now he's free of the pain and suffering of all those years of being abandoned in the orphanage.'

He slowly shook his head as he stared out over the rubbish dump. 'I feel we were just like pieces of garbage dumped by our parents. Nobody cared for us. I was just the lucky one who got out of it.'

As he fell silent, lost in his thoughts, my hand closed round the envelope in my pocket, given to me by Patreascu's adoptive mother Beverly.

For reasons I can't explain, it suddenly seemed exactly the right moment to hand it over to him.

'This contains photos of your mother and father and the name of the village where they live. Beverly tracked them down and kept this for you.'

Without hesitation, Patreascu took the black and white photos out of the package and stared at them, stroking the face of his mother. It was an extraordinary, touching moment, and I had difficulty controlling my own emotions as he told me: 'I want to meet her. This woman carried me for nine months. She brought me into this world. She must have cared for me. But why did she leave me in Ungerini? She has answers I really need right now.'

*

The village where Patreascu's parents lived was just a tiny speck on our map of the Bacau area, suggesting that tracing his family might not be too difficult. It was a good three hours from the city, nestled deep in the mountainous valleys. We decided to head off first thing in the morning, so that when we returned there was no danger of having to drive the mountain roads in darkness. It proved a good decision, as the higher we climbed the more treacherous the route became. The car slid on the icy surface and the driver often swerved to avoid landslides which partly blocked the road. It was not for the faint-hearted: a glance out of the window revealed a stomach-dropping view of the stunning mountain terrain.

Eventually, we descended into a valley and I saw signs of typical gypsy life. Carts pulled by horses and oxen passed by, and wooden homes painted in pastel colours lined the road. The tiny farming community was a world away from life as Patreascu now knew it. As we pulled up, a pack of dogs barked fiercely at the car, drawing attention to our arrival.

Mothers grabbed their children and hurried them nervously inside, while a short, elderly man in tatty clothes came towards us. Despite the freezing temperatures, he had no shoes and was wearing a thin jumper and dirty trousers several sizes too small. His breath stank of alcohol. He swayed as he stretched out to shake our hands – and missed. The interpreter explained to him that we were looking for a family by the name of Nechita. The man froze, stepped back and rubbed his stubbled face as though trying to snap out of his drunken state.

He grabbed Patreascu's face and kissed each cheek passionately, then shouted the same Romanian words over and over again, '*Eu sunt tatăl tău! Eu sunt tatăl tău! Eu sunt tatăl tău!*'

'What the hell is going on?' asked Patreascu, completely bemused. The interpreter placed his hand on Patreascu's shoulder: 'This man says he is your father.'

It was such a remarkable thing to happen that it was hard to take in. Not only was he the first person we'd encountered in the village, the interpreter hadn't actually mentioned who we were or why we were here. Patreascu screamed: 'Gheorge? Is your name Gheorge?'

'Yes, yes, yes!' he replied.

They grabbed each other, hugging and laughing. 'How did he know who I am?' asked Patreascu, but his father just kept kissing his cheek. Gheorge then turned to all of us, not even noticing the camera filming the reunion, and kissed each of us in turn on the cheek. Patreascu asked repeatedly: 'How did you recognise me?'

The man stroked his son's cheek, gesturing excitedly: 'Look at my face. Who do you see? Who do you look like?'

Patreascu's jaw dropped; the resemblance was staggering. When you looked beyond Gheorge's tired, wrinkled face, you could see all Patreascu's features, especially the big, dark eyes, striking nose, large lips and chiselled chin.

Gheorge's ecstatic mood quickly dissolved away. Something appeared to be very wrong. He hung his head and began sobbing. 'Your mother … your mother and I divorced. There are many things you need to know. We should go to your grandmother's now.'

He led us towards a cluster of houses in a field at the end of a long dirt track. Patreascu remained positive, telling me on camera: 'I suppose my mother lives with my grandparents now. I'm nervous, but after meeting my father I am beginning to realise to expect the unexpected. What has become clear to me is that he has never forgotten me.'

Walking ahead of us, Gheorge greeted an elderly woman. As they chatted, the woman wrapped a thick winter coat around her shoulders and then tied a headscarf neatly around her grey hair. Patreascu strode towards her. 'This must be my grandmother – oh my God!'

As they met, the woman placed her hands on his face and wept. Then a younger woman wearing an apron rushed out of the garden to embrace Patreascu. His face lit up, but the translator explained that it was not his mother: 'She is your Aunty Christina – and your grandfather is inside.'

Gheorge gestured us to follow the emotional women up some steps into a small stone home. It was clean, with whitewashed walls and a solid beamed roof. There were just two rooms, a kitchen and a living area with two beds covered in patchwork quilts. Patreascu's grandfather had been sleeping in one of them and hastily put on his trousers as we piled through the tiny door. Patreascu was amazed. 'It's like a cottage from Hansel and Gretel; I can't believe they all live in this tiny house.'

There was still no sign of his mother Elena. 'Where is my mother?' he asked, his voice full of concern. 'Will I see her today? Is she working? Can we tell her I am here?' But nobody answered.

Instead, his grandmother asked him to sit down on his grandfather's bed. She reached for a pot from the stove and poured some thick brown coffee into small metal cups, handing out one to each of us. Then she grabbed some photos pinned behind a framed painting on the wall, placing two in Patreascu's hand and one against her chest. She launched into prayer as tears flowed down her wrinkled cheeks. Patreascu was bewildered. 'This is my mother – these are photos of her. What is going on? Why the crying?'

His grandmother turned to our interpreter and whispered the answer through her distress. Slowly, the interpreter crouched in front of Patreascu, as if reluctant to give the translation: 'I'm afraid she says your mother is dead.'

I had witnessed many emotions from Patreascu over recent days, but his reaction to this news was the most heartbreaking of all. He bowed his head and sobbed uncontrollably, almost destroying the photos of his dead mother as he clenched his hands.

He never told me why he cried so much for a mother he hadn't known. Eventually, his grandmother wiped away his tears and explained everything he had come to hear. 'You were a very sick baby. We had no money for medicines. Leaving you at birth in the hospital was the most difficult decision of your mother's life. They moved you to Ungerini which was a hundred and sixty kilometres from here, and we had no transport except for a horse and cart.

'She thanked God because she knew you would be taken care of, and then you found a better family. But her heart hurt like yours. Her last words before she died were: "It is not God's will for me to see Patreascu again."'

He stared at the photo of his birth mother, brushing the tears from his face. At last he knew that his mother had abandoned him out of love and not neglect. But she was a mother he would now never know. 'I wish I had come sooner. I regret putting this off for so long. She just tried to do the right thing … she did do the right thing. I would love to have told her that.'

Patreascu and his family picked wild flowers from the yard and made their way towards the local cemetery. Visiting the grave of his birth mother was not how Patreascu had ever imagined his journey ending. 'There is so much I wanted to tell her. I wanted her to know about all the wonderful things I have been able to do with my life because I was adopted.'

He kissed the photo of his mother attached to her gravestone. 'I understand now that she had no choice abandoning me. It is the Romanian government that condemned me, not her.'

Despite some almost unbearably poignant moments during his return to Romania, the journey had at last given Patreascu answers to fundamental questions which, deep down, had affected him his entire life. Although I'd only known him for a few days, I could see he was already a changed person, less angry and troubled.

Before we left the village of his birth, he had made an important decision. 'I want to go to the European Union debate with you, Chris. I want the politicians to put down their laptops, throw away their statistics and listen to what someone who has gone through institutionalisation and adoption has to say. If I have to beg the EU to allow adoption again, I will.'

It seemed like the entire village turned out to wave goodbye to Patreascu. Word had soon spread that Elena's son did return after all. And he left with the most powerful of stories, one I was confident he would be able to tell in person at the EU. We were all emotionally drained by the time we got back to the hotel, looking forward to winding down before heading home the next day. But something was wrong: the receptionist was arguing with her manager and our names were being mentioned.

I noticed that the entire team's luggage was piled up in the lobby. When I asked what was going on, the receptionist grabbed my hand,

UNDER COVER

Photographic Documentation

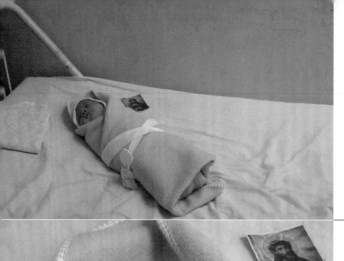

An abandoned baby
left by its mother in a
Romanian hospital.

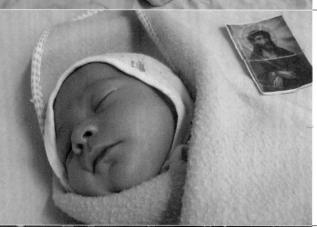

This baby was left with a
note from its mother
'Please God look after
my baby.'

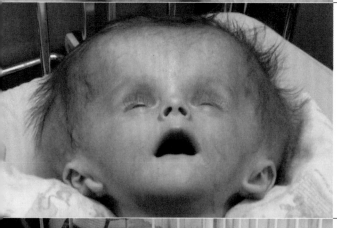

A toddler with hydrocephalus,
abandoned because his
parents did not want to
take care of him. A simple
operation may give him the
chance of a normal life.

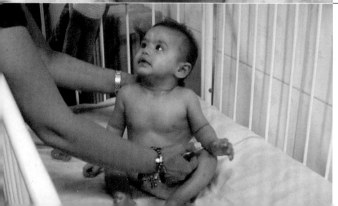

At eighteen months old this
abandoned baby is unable
to sit up, crippled as a result
of being laid down in a cot
all his life.

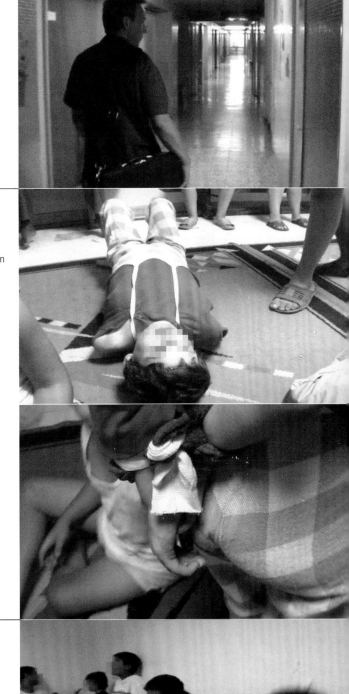

Chris Rogers undercover, posing as an aid worker on a maternity ward full of abandoned children.

Marin Pazon: many children become mentally ill or physically disabled after years in the institution. Some are tied up because of their erratic behaviour (and below).

Marin Pazon: children rocking back and forth, a side effect of institutionalisation.

Marin Pazon: a child is hit by an overwhelmed nurse.

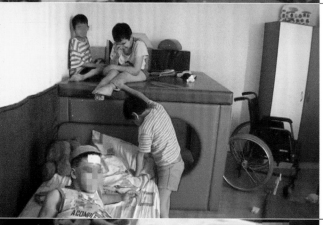

Family-type home: smaller groups of unwanted children are housed here, but despite the comfortable beds and fresh paint, there is still a shocking standard of care.

Family-type home: this boy has his hands tied to a chair 24/7 because he is blind.

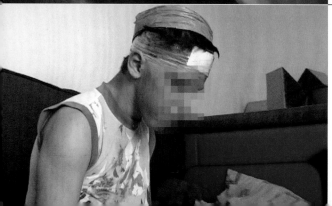

This sixteen-year-old girl has a bandage taped around her head because she keeps falling over. She cannot walk because she has never been taught to.

Chris Rogers in the EU chamber to present his evidence, filmed for *ITV News*.

The Commissioner for EU Expansion dodges Chris's questions as he leaves the chamber, but soon after is presented with the evidence from the investigations.

Romanian Television reports on the *ITV News* investigation. It was their lead story (and below).

Bogdan Paniat on Romanian Television. He claimed the images in the *ITV News* investigation were seventeen years old.

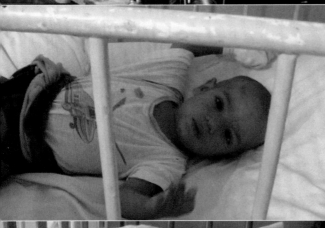

An abandoned baby in a hospital: nurses use T-shirts as nappies. It is illegal to institutionalise children under the age of three, but Romanian hospitals act as orphanages.

Babies abandoned in Romanian hospitals are often left to try to feed themselves.

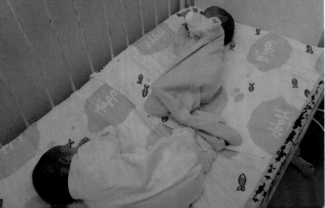

Two abandoned babies share a bed.

Model Lisa B holds a very thin little boy, abandoned by his mother because she could not afford to feed him. He died two days later.

Abandoned babies: many are left in hospital at birth and stay there until they can be put into a State home (and below).

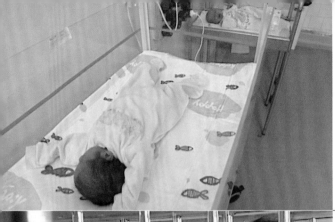

This hospital in Oradea has up to eighty unwanted babies.

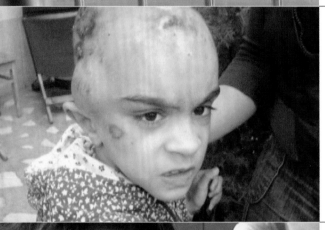

Abandoned children at Brasov Hospital. They should be with foster parents within six weeks of abandonment. Some of these children are nearly three years old.

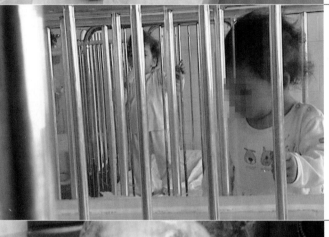

Lydia was tied to her cot in a State orphanage for all nine years of her life. Her head was battered and bruised from years of banging her head against a wall out of loneliness.

Lydia, now at Sarah Wade's home.

This abandoned premature baby, born to a thirteen-year-old mother, is put on the only ventilator at the Oradea children's hospital. But two hours after we filmed this image, the nurses removed the extremely sick baby from the machine and left it to die, making way for another premature baby with a greater chance of survival.

Ungerini Orphanage in the early 90s (and below: photos taken by Beverly Peberdy).

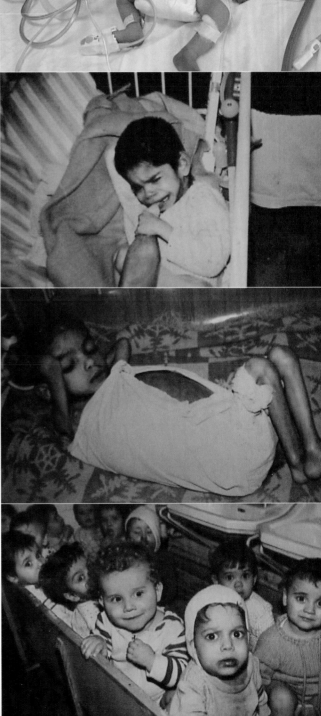

Patreascu and Iulien share
a cot in the dying room.

Beverly in the dying room.

Beverly and John bring
Patreascu to the UK
for surgery.

Ungerini 2007: the children
have remained there for so
long it's now reclassified as
an adult institution.

Ungerini is severely run down after years of neglect. Patreascu knew he could easily have spent his whole life here.

The young adults have been scarred by years of neglect (and below).

Chris and Patreascu at Iulien's grave.

Patreascu is told by his grandmother that his birth mother is dead.

Patreascu weeps as he learns that his mother had never forgotten him.

EU debate on the investigations: The EU concluded that the ban on international adoption should be reviewed and Romania's child welfare would be monitored.

Chris Rogers at the EU debate on his investigations.

MEPs and experts at the debate are visibly moved as they watch the ITV News investigations.

Bogdan Panait and other Romanian officials at the EU debate.

Beverly (left) and Patreascu (second left) look on as Romanian officials storm out of the EU debate in protest at Chris's latest reports.

Patreascu at the EU debate.

Chris negotiates the sale of Monica on the streets of Iyash.

The Duchess of York and Chris Rogers watching his investigations in the ITV newsroom. Sarah travelled with Chris to Turkey and Romania for a special ITV documentary on the continuing plight of unwanted children.

The box specially built by carers to confine Max, who was said to be hyperactive. He left the box for just one hour a day.

Marin Pazon: Three years after Chris exposed this institute, the Duchess and Beatrice find nothing has changed.

A girl tied to a wheelchair.

The nurses try to untie the children, hoping we have not noticed the cruel practice.

Sarah and Beatrice are overwhelmed by children wanting a hug and love at Marin Pazon.

Sarah and Eugenie in an Istanbul institution. This girl has her arms tied to her chest with a jumper.

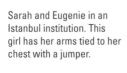

Turkey: Eugenie bursts into tears after her visit to a children's institute in Istanbul.

The Duchess disguises herself as an aid worker to try to get into the Saray Institute in Ankara, Turkey.

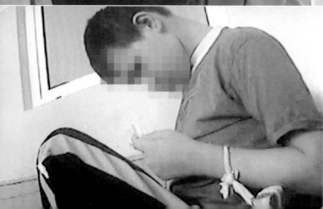

Saray Institute: many adults and children are tied like animals (and below).

whispering to me: 'You and your friends have to leave now. The secret police are looking for you, and they are coming here to search your room and arrest you.' I was gobsmacked, but hugely grateful that the hotel was tipping us off and helping us get away.

Later, it emerged that staff at Ungerini had spotted our big camera filming across the valley and had immediately informed the police. It had been uncharacteristically careless of us to film openly so close to one of our undercover operations.

We grabbed our bags and fled, driving all the way to Bucharest. I was worried that we might be stopped at any time, especially in the airport, but we managed to get on the next flight to London without further incident. As Bucharest shrank away below, I sank into my seat with relief and exhaustion, aware of just how lucky we had been. It was a timely reminder of the risks we ran every time we filmed undercover – we couldn't afford to let our guard down for a moment.

*

Few teenagers have stood in an EU debating chamber and addressed members of the European Parliament. But then few teenagers have a story like Patreascu's. He slowly walked down the aisle and took his seat alongside some of the powerful European Commissioners who would be presiding over the debate. He would be the last one to speak.

The immense circular chamber was nothing if not intimidating. Beneath the flags of every member nation, more than a hundred MEPs took their places, reaching for headphones to hear the debate translated into their native language. With some satisfaction I spotted the Romanian government team, summoned to attend as a result of my reports. A mass of photographers, television cameramen and journalists scrambled for a place in the press pen.

The lights dimmed and two large screens rolled down from the chamber ceiling. The proceedings began with a viewing of my investigations into Romanian orphanages and gypsy villages. I felt a great sense of pride as my work echoed round the Parliament building. Some MEPs covered their mouths in horror at the distressing images, others were openly in tears. In contrast, the Romanian ministers feigned a complete lack of interest, pointedly avoiding watching any of the reports.

The atmosphere was highly charged as the panel of Commissioners asked me to expand on my findings.

'Why did you film secretly?' one asked.

'We would never have been able to film openly in institutions where children are neglected,' I replied, aware of the eyes of the Romanian delegation on me. 'We would have been shown only showcase homes like the ones the EU Commission sees.'

I went on to explain that we visited fifteen institutions in all, during an undercover filming trip four weeks earlier. Unwisely, the Romanian minister Bogdan Paniat interrupted, repeating his slanderous accusation that I'd used old footage to make Romania look unfit for European politics.

'You're doing a good enough job of that yourself,' I responded.

A Commissioner duly took the minister to task, stating that it was insane to accuse a credible news organisation of using old images, and insisting Bogdan Paniat retracted his accusations immediately.

A host of expert witnesses followed, presenting statistics and charts on the emotional and physical effects of institutional care, and debating the merits and dangers of international adoption.

Then, finally, it was Patreascu's turn to speak. As he stood to address the chamber, my heart raced with nerves for him. He had bought a new suit and chopped off his long locks for the occasion, but he still looked far too young to be there.

'In 1992, I became one of an estimated thirty thousand Romanian children adopted by foreigners before my country outlawed the practice. Last week I returned to visit my Romanian orphanage for the first time. Looking around the dormitory of what was once my home triggered long-buried memories of my own desperate childhood. My mother was too poor to take care of me and had left me there thinking I would be better cared for. But I wasn't – I was simply left by the staff in a room to die.'

The MEPs were transfixed, hanging on his every word.

'Sixteen years have passed since I left Ungerini, but nothing has changed. The care is still terrible. I have heard people talk about the importance of staying in Romania for ethnic and cultural reasons. These words are meaningless when you are lying in a filthy rusty cot, waiting for a Romanian foster parent that never comes. They rock all day and all night in their loneliness.

'The only difference is that they have become adults, because they have been there so long. Why? Because nobody comes any more to rescue them. Why? Because adoption is banned. I beg the Romanian government to allow foreign adoption again, to create another form of escape from the misery of institutional care. You are about to see my story, which will be broadcast on ITV and CNN this evening.'

The Romanian delegation had not been warned in advance about this, and as the lights dimmed once more, a journalist from the press pen tapped me on the shoulder, smiling: 'Enjoy this, Chris, it's a rare opportunity to watch the Romanian reaction.'

The secretly filmed images of Patreascu's poignant journey filled the screens. I glanced over at the Romanian team who were in a state of complete panic and confusion. Bogdan Paniat slammed his headphones down. Theodora Bertzi, the Secretary of State for Adoptions, angrily began making calls on her mobile, even though the use of phones in the chamber is banned. Finally, some of the delegation stormed out in protest.

The film ended with Patreascu at his Romanian mother's grave, then reunited in the arms of Beverly and John at his home in Cyprus. The chamber exploded into applause, with every single MEP rising to their feet. I joined them, proud to have witnessed the completion of Patreascu's staggering transformation: from the emotionally detached boy I met in the hotel bar to the impassioned campaigner – a lone voice speaking out for every child who had lived and died in an institution.

*

Patreascu had played a key role in changing hearts and minds and, with it, European policy. Within a week, the European Commission announced a full review of international adoption rules across Europe. It also withdrew its assessment that Romania's child welfare system was now one of the best in Europe. While the country would, as expected, still be allowed to join the EU, it would have to open its doors to regular inspection of all its orphanages to check on progress.

The whole episode was a major humiliation for a proud nation and could have been largely avoided if, instead of cover-ups and lies, it had only acknowledged that it was struggling to cope with the huge issue of abandoned children. It was perhaps not surprising that the very government which got Romania into the EU was voted out of office in the country's national elections just a few months later.

I felt great hope that life could at last be starting to change for the many thousands of children and adults still living a sub-human existence in Romanian institutions. But the battle wasn't quite over yet. Having seen the awful conditions firsthand, I knew it wasn't going to happen overnight.

CHAPTER SIX
LIFE IS CHEAP

As I walked into a busy Tube station in London, I suddenly heard my name bellowed out in a strong East European accent: 'Chris Rogers? Hello Chris Rogers! It is Chris Rogers from *ITV News*, yes?'

Caught off-guard, I was immediately gripped by fear; I had good reason to be wary of anyone from Eastern Europe approaching me out of the blue. To my relief, the stranger reached out to shake my hand, adding enthusiastically: 'I watch you all the time on the television, Chris Rogers.'

I was now a little embarrassed at being recognised. 'Hello, how are you?' I responded with a smile. As we shook hands, I felt the man slip something into my palm, but before I could react he abruptly pulled away and ran off.

In my hand I found a small piece of crumpled paper, with a chilling message scrawled on it: 'We are watching your every move.'

I knew exactly what the note meant and I was terrified. My latest undercover operation had just been broadcast across the globe, exposing the Mafia-like underworld of the East European gangs who force young women and children into prostitution.

Now those same gangs were clearly onto me. Breaking into a cold sweat I nervously looked around, half-expecting to see a gunman or a bunch of heavies about to bundle me into a van. As I scanned wave after wave of commuters pushing past me, I forced myself to calm down, telling myself that the note was probably no more than a warning to back off. But it was also a stark reminder that I had made dangerous enemies in the seedy world where I had spent the last six months.

The investigation started in Romania, a country where I had already discovered life is cheap. My previous reports into the mistreatment of

Romanian children had made a real impact, and reform was promised under the new EU umbrella. But there was an outstanding issue which continued to disturb me. I had been left haunted by images of the children who had been offered to me for illegal adoption, often for no more than the price of a secondhand car. Not one of the gypsy parents involved had questioned my motives, and I kept coming back to the thought that I could easily have been a trafficker or paedophile.

My concerns were heightened a few months later in August 2007 by a United Nations report which stated that Romania had become one of the main sources of women and children for sex trafficking across Europe. Part of the reason, the report concluded, was the relaxation of Romania's borders since it had become an EU member at the start of the year. My mind was made up. While I didn't exactly relish returning to a country where I could face immediate arrest, this was a story I felt compelled to investigate further.

Once again, I teamed up with cameraman Tony Hemmings, aware that, more than ever before, his undercover acting skills would be critical to the safety and success of our mission. This time we would not be posing as innocent aid workers but as the very men we were setting out to expose – traffickers.

*

We decided this time that our best chance of getting into Romania was by car, but the closer we got to the border the more tense I became. Driving towards a country where I was at best *persona non grata*, I began to wonder what on earth I was letting myself in for. However, the very same lack of border controls which allowed the traffickers to operate so freely also worked in our favour, and we slipped into the country completely unchecked.

My first priority was to prove the existence of the under-age sex trade, and it seemed to me that the best place to start my investigation was beneath the streets of the capital Bucharest. More than a decade earlier, my first ever TV report from Romania had featured the desperate plight of the capital's so-called 'sewer children', living below ground in sub-human conditions, sniffing glue to relieve their constant hunger. Many had fled from notorious orphanages or from family abuse, and it was hugely depressing that, ten years on, there were still hundreds of children living like rats.

They were easy prey for traffickers, and I was keen to hear if any had had close encounters with the sex trade. I contacted the aid worker Gabi who'd helped me in 1996. To my relief, he still worked for the same Romanian charity, helping provide the children with basic needs: food, clothes and, when possible, a bed. Gabi used to be a street kid himself and knew nearly every child by name; more importantly they trusted and respected him.

Bearing food and drink to break the ice, Gabi took us to the Gara de Nord train station where most of the street children hang out by day. It's a huge communist-style terminal, surrounded by a neglected park where the homeless laze around or beg. Tony's camera instantly attracted the attention of a gang of teenagers and younger children, all of them apparently high on glue. They screamed and shouted at the camera, one minute waving excitedly, the next angrily telling us to leave them alone. It was quite intimidating, but Gabi quickly calmed them down.

One of the older street children smacked the heads of the younger kids to help bring them under control, before politely introducing herself as Maria. At first I thought she was a boy: she had short black hair, a filthy face and hands, and her body was wrapped in a thick woollen jumper which she had stretched over her ragged jeans. Her eyes latched onto the water and loaves of bread we were carrying; anticipating a meal, she invited us in broken English to her 'home'. At night, whole communities of street children bed down in the network of sewers below the capital, which also carry many of the city's communal hot water pipes. While these scalding hot pipes provide vital heat during the freezing Romanian winter, they are unbearable in the summer. Nevertheless, the sewer kids use the tunnels to sleep in all year round, considering them safer than spending the night at street level.

One by one, we lowered ourselves into the manhole leading to Maria's home. It was late summer and, in the heat, the stench of rotting food and body odour overwhelmed me. Rats ran across my path as I made my way down a dark tunnel lit with candles and littered with empty food cartons. In the flickering light, Maria introduced me to two other girls and five boys she shared the tunnel with. They were all so high on glue none of them seemed able to talk.

I concentrated on chatting to Maria, and my instincts about the sordid life of the street kids were quickly confirmed. She told me she had fled from an institution and had lived on and off the streets since she was nine. When I asked her what she meant by 'on and off', she sighed deeply and began her chilling story. 'A man – a nice man – offered me a room to sleep in and three meals a day if I worked for him. I was so hungry and tired, how could I say no? In a way I knew what the work would be. I knew he would want me to have sex either with him or with other men. But I was so hungry. To start with he was really nice to me and I ate lots of food, and the apartment was OK. But then he began to bring the men … '

Maria looked around the dimly-lit tunnel to make sure the other children weren't listening. 'At first, I refused to have sex with them but he threatened and beat me. I didn't want to go back to the streets and, after a while, I got used to the sex. He kept all the money but, if I behaved, he was nice to me. Then one night he tried to hand me over to another man: he was selling me. I got really scared and ran out of the apartment. So here I am. Back here.'

Almost as shocking as the story was the fact that Maria's tone was so matter of fact, as if what happened to her was the most ordinary, routine thing. Perhaps for the children of the sewers it was. 'The pimp still looks for me. I have gone back to him a few times to get food and sleep. But that was a long time ago.'

Gabi told me he had heard similar heartbreaking accounts, not just from girls but also boys on the street. 'Many children I know have disappeared. A few have been taken by the police and placed back in the institutions or with their parents, but others we fear the worst for.'

We left Tony to film the children bedding down for another night in the stinking sewer. As we returned to street level, Gabi and I chatted about my investigation, prompting him to make an unexpected suggestion. 'We have an ex-trafficker working as a volunteer for us. He's on parole and, as part of his rehabilitation, he has to work with the street children. I could ask if he is willing to speak to you.'

I didn't hesitate in encouraging Gabi to make this happen. I felt it could provide a real insight into the workings of the under-age sex slave industry, and would also help Tony and me to slip into character more easily for the next part of our investigation – the attempt to 'buy' a young girl, ostensibly to work in a British brothel. Gabi immediately called the former trafficker and arranged for us all to meet the next morning. It was to prove a foolish mistake.

*

Stephan looked every bit the low-life you would expect. Catching me staring at his face, he laughed and told me that his false eye and heavy scars were the price he paid for his work: 'You make few friends in my world and many enemies.' I was expecting him to demand money for the interview but he didn't, explaining instead that this was his way of proving to himself and the authorities that he was a changed man. He had just served a typically short sentence in a Bucharest jail for trafficking, and insisted Tony filmed him from behind to hide his identity.

On camera, we talked first about how the market had changed. Stephan had begun by catering only for the local Romanian elite, but more recently he'd started selling girls to foreign gangs. 'Foreign currency gives you credibility,' he told me. 'Now everyone is learning English so we can do business with foreign traffickers. Many are from England, Germany or Italy. But you have to keep finding girls to replace the ones you've sold.'

When I asked him if he ever used street children like Maria in his trade, he laughed, as if to suggest it was a no-brainer. 'Oh yes. To pick up a girl like that you simply make a deal. You offer her a better way of living but tell her she has to prostitute herself.'

His final revelation was even more disturbing. 'You get a lot of requests for young girls and boys from paedophiles. There is a local and international market for nine or ten-year-olds upwards.'

Stephan's account made me even more determined to go through with the long-term 'purchase' of an under-age girl, the most crucial – and dangerous – part of our investigation. To achieve this, we teamed up with a local charity, Reaching Out Romania, which was involved in rescuing young girls enmeshed in the sex trade. Distasteful though it was, they had found that buying the girls off local traffickers was the only sure way to effect a rescue. We travelled back to Bucharest to meet the expert team they'd put together for us.

As ever, the detail of the operation was thrashed out and run past an *ITV News* lawyer and safety officer. Tony and I would lead the investigation by posing as British brothel owners looking for girls to buy and take back to the UK, while one of the team members, John, would act as our 'translator/fixer'. The rest of the team, including an *ITV News* producer, were to stay in the van, monitoring our movements on an open mobile phone line. If we got into any kind of trouble they would sweep in, hopefully managing to extract us before things turned too nasty. If either Tony or I felt uncomfortable at any point, we would simply say that we were 'thirsty'; if we wanted out immediately, we would say we were 'hungry'. In the event that we succeeded in our transaction, others were on hand to care for the girl concerned and take her to safety.

John pulled out two small bottles of whisky. 'Take these with you and swig them. Perhaps smoke some cigarettes and offer them out to break the ice. You'll look less suspicious smelling of alcohol and tobacco.'

We drove into the suburbs, sipping the whisky, which had a great effect on our nerves. John knew of three brothels in one street. 'These places we are about to go into are teeming with girls. They are well known to the locals. But there is also a lot of activity among internal and foreign traffickers swapping and selling girls. They get busy, so be on your guard.'

Having checked the hidden cameras were recording, we jumped out of the van. Lighting cigarettes, we made our way towards the first brothel. It looked like an ordinary, single-storey home, but was surrounded by a high metal fence. The entrance was guarded by two heavily built men. As we approached they blocked our way, refusing to let us in. John didn't hesitate in leading us away: 'They say there are no girls here tonight. This is strange. Let's go to the next one.'

Again it was just an average-looking home, the only give-away being the guarded entrance. And once again we were turned away. John was becoming suspicious. 'Something's up. I have never known these places to be shut – and why would they have guards if they were?' At the third brothel John argued that he had foreign visitors with him with money to spend, but to no avail. As we headed back to the van Tony wondered aloud if we had been rumbled. With a sick feeling in my stomach, I immediately thought of Stephan. When I told John we'd interviewed a former trafficker that morning, he confirmed the stupidity of what we had done. 'This is a small world; everyone looks out for everyone. Of course he has tipped people off. We are screwed now – nobody will let foreigners into their brothels!'

I was so angry with myself; the interview had compromised our entire operation. We decided to call it a night, but our troubles were far from over. As we headed back into the city centre, our driver alerted us that we were being followed. I glanced through the back window to see a black Jeep close behind. According to our driver, it had been trailing us for the whole journey. We swerved into the back streets but the Jeep stayed on our tail. There was no way our bulky van could shake off the 4x4, so our driver decided it was best to head to the nearest hotel, hoping it would trick them into believing we were staying there. With luck, it would also provide a safe haven until we could decide what to do next. We pulled into the car park of the Marriot Hotel and dashed inside. The Jeep parked up but thankfully nobody got out.

As the seriousness of our situation sank in, I wondered if this time I had bitten off more than I could chew. Fortunately, John seemed to take it all in his stride, suggesting that we get out of Bucharest as soon as possible and head north to a city called Iyash. 'We are exposed here but Iyash is a twelve hour drive away. Stephan is unlikely to have contacts there so we should have better luck.'

Iyash is close to Moldavia in a very poor part of Romania and, according to local media reports, trafficking had become rife as a means to make money. We all agreed it made sense to go there and alerted London to our proposed change of plan. After an anxious hour lying low, we saw the Jeep pull away. We decided to risk heading back to our hotel to collect our belongings and filming equipment, and to our great relief the Jeep didn't reappear. We packed our bags and headed north immediately, catching sleep on the way.

*

The long journey proved well worth it. On arrival in Iyash, we enlisted the help of a local taxi driver, and it took us just twenty minutes to encounter a young prostitute called Monica. She was standing outside a petrol station on a busy road, like a piece of meat to sample or buy. Her piercing dark eyes were haunting, and the resigned expression on her face spoke volumes. She was pretty and child-like, but with the hardness of an unloved, empty soul. Her hair was greasy and tangled and her skin dirty and bruised. She told me she was sixteen but looked much younger.

It seemed the most unlikely place to find the under-age sex trade in full flow, but the taxi had brought us straight here. John had rightly judged that, as in many parts of the world, taxi drivers are the best sources of information about the sex industry, paid by the pimps to lead punters to them.

Two hard-faced, middle-aged women were pimping Monica outside the petrol station. They didn't seem surprised to see foreigners approaching them and beckoned us over, out of sight of the CCTV cameras dotted around the forecourt – though of course we were wearing hidden cameras to expose their human trade.

Swigging whisky and smoking heavily to look the part, we made small talk to ease our way in. But the pimps seemed to want to speed things along, perhaps because we were so exposed on the open street. Towering over Monica, they told us: 'You can take her for one hour, a night or for a week – it's up to you.'

Tony coolly stepped in. 'We want to take a girl to Britain for good to work there, so you are no good to us.' His offhand attitude seemed to convince the pimps of his trafficking credentials. One of the women looked down at Monica and smiled. 'OK, you can take her, but I must check with someone first.'

As she made a call on her mobile, John ushered Tony and me away from them and whispered: 'They say she is sixteen but I suspect she is younger. Whatever her age, she looks very ill and we need to give her a chance to get out of this situation. We should definitely rescue her.'

A few minutes later, a black BMW with tinted windows pulled up onto the forecourt and both women began to talk to the driver inside. John later explained it was almost certainly Monica's overall 'owner'. To my utter astonishment, we managed to negotiate a price of just eight hundred euros to 'buy' Monica for good. I tried to remain cool, as if purchasing a young girl was something I did every day, but it was all I could do to stay in character. As John counted out the cash, I felt my stomach tightening. How could a child's life be so cheap?

You would expect any girl to be terrified as they are taken away by strangers, but Monica seemed to accept her fate completely. I got the distinct impression this was by no means the first time this had happened to her. We piled into the taxi and sped off.

The secret footage we had gathered would later prove invaluable in raising awareness of the terrible trade but, at that moment, the success of the mission was far from my mind. I was shaking with adrenaline and wanted to be sick. Despite my good intentions for Monica – and the many other young girls in similar dire circumstances – I felt like I had just committed an awful crime. I was desperate to tell her the truth, but had been advised to leave this to John and his team.

We pulled into a car park, paid the taxi driver a good tip, and escorted Monica into our van, where the rest of the team had been waiting. As we headed out of Iyash for what would be yet another long drive, Monica turned to me and offered me sex. I should of course have anticipated that this might happen – perhaps her former owner expected it – but I was completely taken aback and hit by a fresh wave of nausea.

The charity team stepped in to reveal our true identities to Monica, explaining that we were taking her to a charity-run safe house which looked after victims of sex trafficking. If I was expecting gratitude, I was in for quite a shock. Monica screamed and cried hysterically, hitting out at me. Then, like a wounded child, she curled up into a ball and sobbed, shaking with emotion.

John explained that it was a typical reaction. Adults had let Monica down so completely for most of her young life that she didn't know what to think. Over and over, he reassured her that the charity would take care of her and, if she wished, her testimony could eventually put her traffickers behind bars and help rescue many more girls trapped in the country's illegal brothels.

Eventually, she snuggled up to me and asked for a cigarette. Between sobs, she began to tell me more about her background, a story so appalling that it was hard to see how she could ever trust an adult again. She explained that her parents sold her to the traffickers when she was nine. 'I was then sold on to another gang and taken to Bucharest. I didn't know where I was heading but I didn't like them, so I ran away.'

She lit another cigarette with her shaking hands. 'I got to a government safe house for street kids and trafficking victims, but I was abused there so I ran off, escaping through the window. As I headed back to Iyash, I was picked up by the police. They put me in the back of a van and beat me. They even filmed it for their pleasure. Eventually they let me go and I went back to the people you found me with.'

She saw the look of confusion on my face and added: 'I went back to what I knew best.'

It was hardly surprising she was reluctant to believe what this new day offered her.

The Reaching Out Romania safe house was in a secret location, to protect the girls who lived there from the traffickers they'd escaped. Run by Iana Matie, a fearless woman who often speaks out against traffickers to the international media, the project had already helped more than a hundred girls with counselling, education and long-term support.

Iana was waiting for us in the doorway, ready to welcome Monica to what we all hoped would be her new home. Iana hugged her like a mother, then led her to the interview room where all rescued victims are taken for immediate counselling. An hour later, Monica emerged tired but relaxed and kissed each one of us on the cheek as she headed to bed.

Iana told me that this could be the start of a new life for her, but only if she chose to accept it. 'Monica can experience something here she has never known: trust, love and understanding. She is not stupid; she knows she has a chance here. But it's a long and fragile process.'

Dealing with such damaged young girls, the project didn't have a hundred per cent success. 'She may go back to her traffickers and we have to accept that. We don't want her to, but she fears them and, at the same time, they are all she knows. Why should she trust me or you when everyone who offered her help before, like the police and the staff of the government safe house, have let her down and abused her?'

Next day, we returned to the charity safe house to say goodbye to Monica. She had new clothes on and had befriended some of the other girls. I was moved to discover she had already taken part in an art class, and had painted a picture of herself for Tony and me to take away. As she handed it over, she promised us she would give her new life a chance. It was the first time I had seen her smile.

*

We had captured on camera the chilling ease with which under-age girls like Monica are traded like cattle and, over the coming months, I followed the trail of trafficked girls across Europe. Slipping ever deeper into my role as a British trafficker, I even set up a website for a fake London brothel called EU-rotica, supposedly catering for the tastes of men who like young Eastern European girls.

Working undercover as a buyer for EU-rotica, I discovered that many Romanian orphans and street kids are sold on to Prague in the Czech Republic, a city with the dubious honour of being dubbed 'Europe's brothel'. I was now rubbing shoulders with powerful international gangs who coordinated the trafficking of hundreds of young girls. I couldn't afford the slightest slip and was advised to change my appearance to look more like a typical brothel owner. I spiked my hair, bought a garish gold chain and pierced my ear, inserting a diamond stud.

My cameraman Tony was bulky enough to play the role of my security guard, and we arranged to meet gang members to stock up our fake brothel. We knew that, in this Mafia-like world, we had to be prepared for body searches, so we hid our secret recording kit in well-padded jacket collars and pockets, meticulously sewing the wires into the coat's lining. As we headed to the meetings, I prayed that the intense fear I was feeling wasn't too apparent.

Our preparations paid off. We caught on camera several key players in the international sex trade, and gathered firm evidence that Prague is not only a sex tourist favourite, but also a major supply route for brothels in Britain.

To complete the grim picture, I wanted to show on camera that under-age girls from Eastern Europe were indeed ending up in the UK. Tony and I devised a simple strategy: we would pose as potential punters, targeting some of the many brothels across Britain which advertised East European prostitutes. The aim was to film all we could before making our excuses and leaving, perhaps by one of us pretending to 'lose our nerve'.

While many girls appeared under-age, it was hard to question them to confirm their stories: the Madam or pimp would stand by our side as they showed off the choice on offer. But, finally, we found unequivocal evidence in a huge brothel in Birmingham, where we were offered a choice of fifteen Romanian girls. They paraded into the waiting room in a semi-circle in a well-rehearsed drill. The heavy make-up, high heels and short skirts couldn't hide their thin, child-like frames and young features. It was a room full of Monicas.

*

The evidence I had gathered over the past six months was potentially explosive, exposing powerful criminal gangs and a trail of illegal activity within the European sex trade. Following the discovery of the under-age Birmingham brothel, the *ITV News* editor and I felt that the police now needed urgently to be involved. I contacted the British police operation Pentameter, which co-operates with agencies across Europe to clamp down on trafficking. When I told the head of Pentameter what I had captured on film in Romania, the Czech Republic and Britain, he immediately arranged a meeting at their offices.

I arrived to quite a gathering, including the officer in charge of an undercover operation to crack down on European gangs, executives from British Customs and Immigration, a number of Special Branch officers, and finally, to my horror, a representative of a Romanian special police force, the National Agency against Trafficking, the equivalent of the UK's Pentameter operation.

At first I refused to continue the meeting in his presence, explaining that I had experienced nothing but denials and intimidation from the

Romanian authorities over my investigations. I was, however, assured that he was in Britain co-operating with Pentameter and furthermore that his Agency fully supported my investigation.

I played a selection of footage from the investigative series, which would be broadcast across the globe in just a few days' time. I was slightly apprehensive that such experienced officers might have seen it all before, but they were shocked at the ease of the purchase of Monica and the sheer number of under-age girls caught on film.

The week of broadcast, in January 2008, was to provide some of the greatest highs and lows of my career. As the reports went out, several prominent European traffickers identified on camera were arrested. The Czech authorities announced the permanent closure of many illegal brothels; and the British brothels we had visited were raided, with all the victims we had identified brought to safety, including the fifteen under-age Romanian girls in the Birmingham brothel.

Each day, news reached me of more arrests and brothel raids, and I suspected it was only a matter of time before the men I had exposed would seek some kind of revenge. The frightening note handed to me by an East European man in a London Underground station was just the start of a long campaign of intimidation. I received dozens of threatening phone calls and emails. On the advice of security officers, I took time off work and went into hiding.

At the same time, I also received some bad news about Monica. Iana called me to confirm the outcome we all feared: she had fled back to the city of Iyash. Her two months at the safe house had been an emotional rollercoaster ride. She had made friends with the other girls and received education, love and care for perhaps the first time in her life. But she had been diagnosed with syphilis from years of unprotected sex. Her identity papers had been tracked down, confirming that she was just fourteen years old. I couldn't begin to imagine how she could possibly come to terms with all that had happened to her, and it seemed the emotional scars had proved impossible to heal in such a short time.

Within days, the Chief of Iyash Police, who had been heavily criticised in my investigation, called a press conference and announced a warrant for my arrest for kidnapping. It was a laughable accusation but, in a sickening twist, he issued a filmed statement of a terrified-looking Monica telling the camera that she was in fact twenty-five-years old, and backing up their claims that she had been kidnapped by me.

The move completely backfired. The Romanian media weren't having any of it. The reaction from the newspaper *Romania Libera* was typical, running an article stating that:

```
Chris Rogers was the victim yet again of the
Romanian government and police who refuse to
accept his claims in the face of criticism... To
suggest that an award-winning reporter such as
Rogers held a young Romanian prostitute against
her will for the purpose of his film puts our
country to shame.
```

In the face of mounting criticism, the police Chief was forced to backtrack, admitting he couldn't provide any official evidence of Monica's supposed age. Sources confirmed that the police had picked Monica up on her return to Iyash in a deliberate attempt to discredit my reports.

There was a much more positive response from Romania six months later, when my investigations were shown at a European Union summit on trafficking. The effect of the films was powerful, drawing gasps from the delegates. As promised, the President of Romania's National Agency against Trafficking welcomed the investigations, expressing his shock at what I had uncovered and stating that Romania had to do more to fight human trafficking. And he was as good as his word: in the months that followed, his Agency uncovered dozens of Romanian trafficking operations, rescuing many children along the way.

Sadly, Monica was not among them. Despite pressure from the Romanian authorities, charities and journalists, the Iyash police persistently claimed they had no idea where she was, and she remains missing to this day, one of the countless young victims of the abhorrent trade for whom reform came too late.

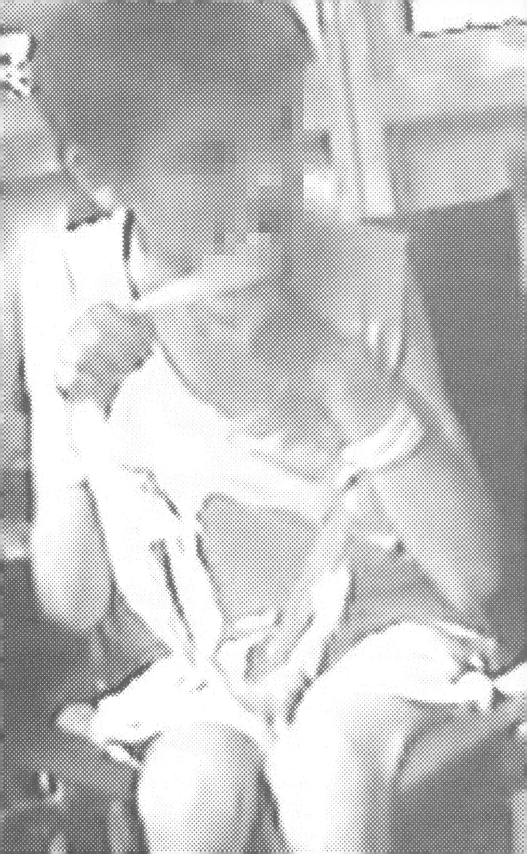

CHAPTER SEVEN

DUCHESS AND DAUGHTERS: THEIR SECRET MISSION

Investigating the plight of abandoned, unwanted children across Europe had dominated my career for five years, and along the way there were other challenging stories. In Far Eastern prisons I uncovered horrific human cruelty and crime; in the Gaza Strip I reported on the realities of life for children on both sides of the conflict, attracting rubber bullets from Israeli soldiers for my troubles; back in the UK I dug beneath the headlines to discover the heart-breaking human cost of a spate of knife and gun attacks on young people.

But shortly after exposing the trafficking of European children, I became involved in an assignment like no other, so unprecedented it had to be kept secret from many of my colleagues, friends and family. Those in the know believed I would never pull it off.

It would take me undercover once more into the familiar, distressing territory of European orphanages: the difference was that this time I hoped to take a duchess and two princesses with me.

After seeing my Romanian reports on TV in 2007, Sarah Ferguson, the Duchess of York, had contacted me with a view to witnessing for herself the bleak places where unwanted children were kept. Her aim was to find and fund solutions, and lend her profile to a cause still greatly in need of further exposure.

During my first, slightly surreal meeting with the Duchess, held at just half an hour's notice behind closed doors in a London hotel, she had made it clear that she was happy for our proposed trip to be filmed to help bring the issues to world attention. But she was keen not to focus on just one country, insisting her campaign was to be for every abandoned child in Europe. So I drafted in the expertise of Eric Rosenthal of the Washington-based lobby group, Mental Disability Rights International, the man who first alerted me to the problems with Romania's institutional care.

On learning about the plans for such a major documentary, he immediately flew from America to London to help thrash out a plan of action. He brought with him another member of the MDRI team, Laurie Ahern: as a former investigative journalist she specialised in collecting evidence of poor care across the globe.

We began by comparing notes on the situation in Romania. It was two years since my last reports – and almost as long since all the positive signs which accompanied the country's entry into the European Union. But according to the aid workers we had spoken to, improvement had been patchy and abandonment was still a massive problem. I confessed to being hugely disappointed with the pace of progress: 'Considering the promises of the EU to monitor Romania's reform of its child welfare system, I expected better news by now.'

It seemed clear to me that we should definitely return to Romania to expose these continuing problems, but as Eric and I talked further, I realised it was going to be easier said than done. 'The greatest change in Romania is getting access to the institutions,' he explained. 'I've been told that orphanage staff have been instructed to watch out for journalists and secret cameras, and to treat all aid workers with suspicion. It's going to be much tougher to get inside these places.'

I knew Sarah was keen to visit the country which had first moved her to get in touch, and would be as incensed as I was that so little had changed. I could only hope that the difficulty of the assignment would not put her off.

But where else should we go as well? Eric told me the issue of abandonment of children was far more widespread than most people imagined:

MDRI had conducted investigations in more than twenty countries, and the United Nations Children's Fund, UNICEF, had recently estimated that there were more than a million institutionalised children across Europe.

We couldn't, of course, highlight every country and every problem in a one hour documentary. Along with Romania, I felt we should concentrate on filming in just one other country that epitomised the widespread issue.

'Then I think we should go to Turkey,' Eric stated without hesitation. 'That country is my greatest concern. While some children there are orphaned, most have been abandoned by their families because there is shame associated with having a disabled child.'

Ironically, Turkey was hoping within a few years to follow Romania into the European Union. Eric handed me a copy of MDRI's report on the country, cautioning that it made grim reading: 'In 2005, MDRI discovered a serious lack of care for abandoned disabled children – so serious that we described the conditions in Turkey's institutions for special needs children as tantamount to torture.'

As a journalist, my initial reaction to this extreme claim was to dismiss it as hype – over the years I have seen so many press releases from charities which 'over-sell' their cause to try to grab headlines. But Eric, a former law professor, went on to explain that this was a charge MDRI didn't make lightly, guiding me through the many breaches by Turkey of human rights legislation designed to protect children.

Laurie backed up Eric's cool analysis with a moving description of what she had seen while she was gathering evidence: 'Imagine being a child kept in the same room, tied to a bed, day after day, week after week, year after year. No fresh air, no daylight and not a single embrace, kiss or bedtime story. Zero attention. You don't need to know your laws to know that it's torture.'

Eric and Laurie expressed their desire to help in any way they could, but pointed out that again it wasn't going to be easy: 'The idea is for MDRI to support governments with our reports, and guide them to better care. But Turkey appears to have simply ignored our findings. Aid workers out there have told us that very little has changed, despite promises by the Turkish government that they would act. In fact, they seem to put most of their energy into punishing aid workers for helping us compile our report. With this sort of intimidation, I can't guarantee that we'll have any charities out there to help us get access to institutions.'

The idea of taking the Duchess with me was getting more daunting by the minute. Heading undercover into foreign orphanages was always a scary undertaking, even for an old hand like myself, and if Eric and Laurie were right it was now going to be harder than ever.

*

It was a make-or-break moment for the project. I feared Sarah might well want to pull out, but when I filled her in on the potential difficulties in gathering the evidence in both countries, she remained the optimist I remembered from our first meeting: 'If what we intend to do is right, if it's meant to be, we'll find a way,' she declared defiantly. 'This is why I need you Chris, the journalist, so Sarah here, the humanitarian, can see the real situation.'

We both knew her involvement could be the difference between a five minute piece on *News at Ten* and a sixty minute documentary broadcast all over the world: 'Of course I will help, I have to,' she continued in typical forthright manner. 'We owe it to the children.'

*

Just a few weeks later came an astonishing addition to the team, in the shape of Sarah's daughters, Beatrice and Eugenie. The two princesses had apparently expressed their desire to join their mother to help her with the campaign. Twenty-year-old Beatrice, the older of the sisters, told me that she had been thinking for some time about following in her mother's footsteps: 'I want to make charity work my mission in life, Chris; my mum has shown me that. Ever since I saw your investigations I've thought that it mustn't stop there. It can't because there are children who need a voice.'

I admired the young generation of Royals for wanting to help, and knew that their involvement in the project could potentially be a huge bonus. It was what I'd always secretly hoped, but it also presented a fundamental problem: unlike their mother, the princesses are full members of the Royal family, grandchildren of Her Majesty the Queen. Visits by Royals to other countries are traditionally publicly announced, high profile events, which meant our filming in institutions would be scuppered – no government would allow Royalty to see neglected children tied to their beds.

I immediately called Sarah, only to find she had already anticipated my concerns. 'For starters, Chris, this is not an official Royal visit – I must make that clear. This is mother and daughters travelling and working together on a personal journey. What's more, the girls are eighteen and twenty now. They think for themselves and this is something they want to do. We are not going to wrap them up in cotton wool.'

ITV executives agreed the only way forward was to take the unprecedented step of making the journey a secret mission, off the radar of the media and all but trusted officials. But success was still far from guaranteed, not least as the movements of the Royals have a habit of leaking to the press. The Yorks were regularly followed by the paparazzi, and if word of the trip got out, it could blow the entire mission. We decided to reduce the risk by taking each princess to only one country: Beatrice would go to Romania and Eugenie to Turkey.

For the first time, I began to believe the shoot might actually go ahead. ITV secretly commissioned a one hour special edition of their flagship documentary series *Tonight*. It would be called: '*Duchess and Daughters: Their Secret Mission*'. The channel's bosses made it clear that if we pulled this documentary off, it would be a television first. More importantly, we hoped that for more than a million children institutionalised across Europe, it would also offer a first glimmer of hope.

The success of the mission depended on meticulous planning, and I ran through every scenario in fine detail with the *Tonight* production team. I would travel ahead of the Duchess and her daughters, posing as an aid worker, looking for institutions that might need charitable help. To make sure my cover was convincing, we set up a website for a bogus charity called The Global Children's Trust, also printing pamphlets and ID cards.

I would visit a number of institutions of concern, and request permission for a visit by donors to my 'charity'. The donors were of course to be the Duchess and her daughters, who we would secretly film looking round the institutions. We hoped they would not be recognised, but in the event that they were, we agreed we would be open about their true identity.

For British broadcasters, secret filming is only sanctioned if it meets strict criteria, primarily that it's the only method of gathering evidence of known wrongdoing, and is also in the public interest. Senior ITV executives and lawyers went over our proposed filming trip, concluding that it was indeed the only way we could expose the awful conditions for children in both countries.

With just two weeks to go to the trip, I was alerted to a story in a gossip column in a British newspaper. To my horror, it had spilt the beans, revealing that according to a 'close source', the Princesses were planning a trip to Romania and Turkey to see conditions inside the countries' orphanages.

The entire production team was devastated; it seemed that months of careful, secretive planning had been wasted. But we decided to press on with the arrangements and hope for the best. By some miracle, the article was not noticed by either country, and not one other paper picked up on the story.

*

September 18th 2008 – a day I witnessed the unthinkable: the Duchess of York and her younger daughter Eugenie stepping off a plane at Turkey's Istanbul airport, and not a photographer in sight.

It was the first time I had met Eugenie. She was strikingly pretty, with thick, dark hair, large green eyes and a huge grin. Like her sister Beatrice, she had clearly inherited her looks from her father Prince Andrew, while her personality seemed a lovely mix of both parents: strong, independent and no-nonsense. I instantly liked her.

My greatest worry was whether the eighteen-year-old would be able to stomach the facility which I had visited just a few hours earlier. The director of the Zeytinburnu Rehabilitation Centre in the suburbs of Istanbul had told me that institutions such as hers were strictly out of bounds to visitors, but using my fake aid worker ID, I had convinced her to show me around.

The Centre was home to around sixty unwanted children, and it quickly became clear why visitors were generally not welcome. The facility had been featured in the damning 2005 report by MDRI, and it appeared conditions had not improved. Children with and without disabilities were housed under the same roof. The rooms were colourful but sparse, with few staff and nothing for the children to do. They all seemed very distressed.

The director of the Centre agreed to my return with potential donors and, having picked up Sarah and Eugenie, we headed straight back. The cameras started rolling, filming everything that happened in 'fly on the wall' style. It was far from the natural environment I would have liked in order to get to know Eugenie, but we could not delay in case word spread that she and her mother were in town.

I asked Eugenie if she was sure she wanted to witness the plight of the children in the Centre. She was determined, telling me she had for a long time been keen to help her mother: 'Look, I know it sounds corny, but all my life my sister and I have shared my mother with the world's children. I admire her for that and I'm proud of her. But life back home is so removed from what goes on around the world. It's hard for me to imagine what she has seen, so this is me wanting to see it for myself.'

As we drove down a back alley leading to Zeytinburnu, we made final checks on our secret filming equipment. Everything would be captured on hidden cameras worn by me, the cameraman Rupert and the director Ruth, who were both posing as my colleagues from our bogus charity, the Global Children's Trust.

The Zeytinburnu Rehabilitation Centre looked like a small run-down school, and in the playground we were immediately greeted by excited children who welcomed us with hugs and kisses. It was only when we got inside that things became more disturbing.

With no apparent interest in our movements from the overworked staff, we began to open doors and investigate further. Sarah spotted a young boy rocking violently in the corner of a room; as we walked towards him, he stopped and held his arms out with his wrists clamped together. 'It looks like he's expecting to be tied up,' Sarah whispered to me, and then we noticed that he seemed to have abrasions on his wrists.

He was not alone: many of the children were covered in sores and scars around their wrists and ankles.

In another room we found a severely disabled girl lying on the floor, dressed with her hands and arms inside her jumper, which was acting as a straight-jacket. A carer confirmed to Sarah that she was always kept like this. Eugenie tried to play with a boy who was sitting motionless on a carpet, but he simply ignored her. When she asked the staff his name, she was shocked to discover that none of them knew it, explaining away this lack of humanity with the fact that he was deaf.

But perhaps most disturbing of all was the repetitive behaviour displayed by so many of the children, the all-too-common sign of complete neglect which I had witnessed so often in recent years. Every corner we turned, we found children endlessly rocking back and forth. When Eugenie and her mother started to play with some of them, I noticed that they immediately stopped the rocking: all the children needed was attention from another human.

It all became too much for Eugenie, who burst into tears and ran outside. We judged it was time for all of us to leave. Sarah immediately went to comfort her daughter, reassuring her that things can change, and that some good had already been done by filming the neglect.

I felt confident she was right: the evidence we had gathered would not only create awareness, it would expose Turkey's breaking of international agreements. The country had signed up to the United Nations Convention on the Rights of the Child, which states that all children have the right to life and development, growing up in an environment of happiness, love and understanding. These basic rights were a far cry from the hopelessness we had just witnessed.

Eugenie sobbed, holding her mother's hand tightly until we reached our van and the rest of the team. As we drove off out of sight of the institution, our bigger cameras came back out. I was concerned that Eugenie might be too emotional to be interviewed, but she insisted, telling me it was an experience that had immediately changed her outlook on life.

'In the hustle and bustle of a cosmopolitan city, in a popular tourist destination, it's hard to comprehend places like that exist. My eyes have been opened.' Tellingly, she wondered if she would ever be able to explain what she had seen to her friends back home. 'I'll try but they probably won't get it. This is something so awful that people who've never seen it for themselves may never truly understand.'

Despite being highly experienced in humanitarian work, Sarah was also shocked, particularly over the housing of disabled and non-disabled children together. 'Being abandoned may just be the start of their problems. For instance, there was one little girl I played with who was completely normal. But she could now end up following her peers and just copying that institutionalised rocking, never really knowing anything except going from room to room.'

'There were some moments that made me angry,' said Eugenie, 'like the staff not knowing the deaf boy's name. How long does it take to learn someone's name? It's just that little bit of kindness that brings a little bit of joy to a boy or girl.' She paused, then added reflectively: 'It brought me joy creating a smile on their faces – it was all I could do.'

This was just the start of Eugenie's eye-opening journey. I wanted to take her and Sarah to another facility I had investigated, which would show there was little chance of escape from institutionalisation for Turkey's disabled.

Earlier that day, I had gone undercover in an adult facility where the patients were kept in one crowded room. I explained to Sarah and Eugenie that what I'd seen was effectively a 'dying room', and that it was where many of the children from Zeytinburnu would end up.

Again, believing I was from a British charity, the director of the institution had agreed to show the potential donors around, admitting that she desperately needed funds to give her patients a better life. On entering the room I had visited earlier, Sarah and Eugenie were horrified by what they encountered. Everywhere they looked, patients lay motionless on crowded benches lining the bare walls. They were all heavily sedated, some resting their numbed bodies on each other. Swarms of flies landed on their shaven heads, or on the saliva streaming from their mouths. The room was lifeless; the only sound came from a television mounted on the wall behind a wire cage, but nobody was watching except a janitor perched on a stool with his back to the mass of bodies behind him.

There seemed to be no distinction between those with mental illness and those with a mild disability; all were kept in the crowded room. The director explained that because she had few staff, she thought it best to keep the patients contained.

'So they spend all day, every day, in this one room with nothing to do?' asked Sarah in disbelief. The director looked ashamed and shrugged her shoulders.

Sarah spotted a man with Down's Syndrome, which seemed to add fuel to her anger at the conditions she was witnessing. I had learnt by now she always spoke her mind, especially where she saw people in need, and despite the risk of blowing our cover, there was no holding her back. 'Do you think that he should be here, or do you think he should not?' she demanded of the director.

'It is hard to explain to foreigners why this happens in Turkey,' the director replied wearily. 'It's complicated.'

We spent an hour in the room, with Sarah and Eugenie desperate to try and engage with the patients. Just like the children at Zeytinburnu, the adults craved physical contact. Eugenie hugged nearly every single one of them, and as she did, tears rolled down her cheeks.

*

I was emotionally drained after all we had experienced in the space of just a few hours, and this, of course, was despite the dubious advantage of having seen it all before. I could only imagine how Eugenie felt, witnessing such distressing, sub-human scenes for the first time. I knew both she and her mother would feel guilty about switching off for the evening and returning to normality, but I could see that they desperately needed a break.

To lift our spirits I booked dinner for all of us in a stunning district of Istanbul called Ortaköy. I knew Istanbul well: as a teenager I had spent several months in the city working for a radio station, and like so many foreign visitors I had fallen for its magic. The city is spread over seven hills and surrounded on three sides by water, its skyline punctuated by ancient mosques and modern skyscrapers. With one foot in Europe and the other across the Bosphorus in Asia, Istanbul offers an exciting taste of both continents.

The city had become far more affluent in the years since I lived there. Ortaköy was now a cool neighbourhood with atmospheric cafes and bistros, and crowds of young, sophisticated residents and tourists. Against this backdrop, our discoveries earlier in the day were profoundly shocking, and despite our best efforts, the conversation soon gravitated back to the institutions.

'I cannot stop thinking about what we do now, how we help,' said Eugenie. 'I knew this trip would involve opening doors to a world I hadn't seen, and I understand that exposing it will to a degree change things, but after you've been in that world, you have to do something, you want to help people. But how?'

I knew how Eugenie felt, and to be honest I had always been thankful to have chosen a career which simply involved exposing problems, rather than trying to fix them. I explained that I could only admire those who attempted such an overwhelming job.

One such person is of course the Duchess of York herself. Sarah was already scribbling notes on potential projects, and calling contacts to try and raise funds for all she hoped to achieve.

'I think we're all attuned together,' she declared. 'What I mean is that this film we are making is not about Beatrice, Eugenie and me; it's about us being really inspired by your work, Chris. We're a great team: you are the exposer, and we are the campaigners. We want to support you and help shed light on the issue. But we can't just leave it at that, we want to create change.'

'Mummy just loves being back in the field – that's what she calls it,' Eugenie added with a smile. 'It's the only place she feels at home.'

Later, Eugenie told me that the experiences she had in Turkey had given her a similar sense of purpose. A welcome side effect was that her fear of the often critical British press was fading.

'I might not seem it, but I'm actually quite a shy person,' she admitted. 'I don't like walking into a room by myself because I'm terrified that people are looking at me. I think it's the press that has made me so insecure. But after what I have seen, the suffering, I'm not really bothered as much about what people think of me.'

I was greatly impressed by her new-found maturity. 'Seeing people in adversity has inspired me to help,' she continued. 'I am more sure of who I am and what I can do. That is all that matters, not what other people think I am.'

*

There was one last institution I wanted to secretly film before leaving Turkey, but it was in a completely different league in terms of the potential dangers. We all agreed that the risks were too great for Eugenie to join us: on this occasion it would be just me and Sarah.

We had heard stories of terrible neglect in a vast institution called Saray, in the country's capital, Ankara. It held a staggering seven hundred unwanted, disabled children, with more buildings being planned to hold hundreds more. Unlike the facilities in Istanbul, Saray was completely shut off to foreign visitors of any kind. It was also heavily guarded.

As with the other institutions, I had attempted to gain access under the guise of our bogus children's charity, writing to the director of Saray claiming we had wealthy donors who wanted to look around. But on this occasion my approach had, not unexpectedly, been turned down.

Eric Rosenthal and Laurie Ahern from MDRI joined us in Ankara to brief us on the institution. They had both been inside Saray before, and in the back of our hired bus, away from prying eyes, Eric drew a map outlining dozens of buildings. Sarah and I were amazed at the sheer size of the place.

Laurie pointed her finger at the entrance. 'You don't have to look far for poor care. This is where they have the administration, and just across the corridor we found very young children, about four, five, six years old, in terrible conditions. Just follow the smell – the stench of faeces was overpowering. It was on the walls and the floor.'

Eric turned back to his makeshift map of the institution. 'Some buildings contain non-severe children, others contain severe. They are the most shocking, as the children are bed-bound.'

Sarah's mouth dropped open. 'What hope is there for these children?' she exclaimed. 'Is it like some kind of prison cell for these kids?'

Eric nodded in agreement, and then pointed in turn at every building he had drawn. 'Every single kid in these buildings has no hope. They will go from a kids' facility to an adult facility – all in the same complex. There is no hope of escape through fostering. That is the Turkish system.'

But proving any of this on film appeared unlikely. With absolutely no access, Sarah and I decided we would boldly turn up at the gate and attempt to bluff our way in. It was, to say the least, a long shot, but having come so far we were determined to give it a go.

Our chance of arrest was high. On an earlier trip, the production team and I were even arrested by the police while filming openly outside. They had insisted on viewing the material we had filmed, which luckily was just a few general shots of the street. Having taken copies of our passports and press ID cards, they let us go.

To help minimise the risks – and maximise our chances of getting in – we agreed that this time Sarah should disguise herself: being recognised at the gate would not be helpful. As the Duchess put on a pair of dark glasses and concealed her 'trademark' red hair with a dark wig, I mentioned the criticism she might face in the press for going to such extreme lengths.

But possible press reaction was of little consequence to Sarah: 'Some say you should worry about what people think of you, and control your spontaneity. I say – do you think a child in there minds if I'm spontaneous? All that child wants is somebody to be its champion. You opened my eyes to it, Chris, and I jumped in; it's just the way I am. Could be the Celtic red-headed Irish in me, I don't know, but all I know is if I was lying in that bed and I knew there was a great, big, old battleaxe like me out there shouting for me, I'd be pretty pleased.'

*

We drove towards the checkpoint at the entrance to Saray. Despite having done this hundreds of times before, I was very nervous: the slightest suspicion and we would without a doubt be reported to the police.

As ever, Sarah looked as cool as a cucumber. It was only much later that she admitted she had never been so scared in her life, constantly recalling nightmarish scenes from the movie *Midnight Express*, based on the true story of an American drug smuggler who was incarcerated in a horrendous Turkish prison. But Sarah knew that her fears of losing her freedom were as nothing compared to the life sentence endured by the children we were about to visit, and it was this thought which drove her on.

I flashed my fake ID with an air of confidence at the uniformed guards, and to our absolute relief we were neither questioned nor turned away. Instead, the guards escorted us to the director's office. But as we were heading there, disaster struck: a belt holding the recording equipment for my hidden camera suddenly broke, and the recorder fell down my trouser leg. Still attached to wires, it hung just above my ankle. I couldn't take another step without the guards noticing.

My instinctive reaction was to pretend to have severe stomach cramps and nausea, and request an urgent visit to the toilet. Looking back, it was almost farcical, but it did the trick. The bemused guards pointed me in the direction of the nearest convenience. I held my stomach, and by crouching in apparent pain I managed to grab the wires, stopping the equipment falling any further as I edged down the corridor.

The Duchess, who obviously realised something serious was up, kept the guards talking while I got my act back together in the cubicle. It was a very close call, and my heart was still racing as we entered the office area.

Our extraordinary lucky streak continued. Not only was the overall director away for the day, the assistant director had no issue in allowing us to tour the institution. All became clearer when he explained that he was being removed from his post: 'I am being moved to a remote institution on the border. I think this may be because I have created too many waves: I wanted to allow foreign charities to have significant involvement here but this has been refused.'

It seemed he had expressed his frustration at the lack of resources once too often. Allowing us in was perhaps his final act of defiance. 'Not all you will see is good here, but we try to cope,' he said despondently.

Two Turkish aid workers and a member of staff ushered us into a large, sparsely decorated room. The stench of urine, sweat and vomit that hit us as the doors opened was all too familiar to me. I should have been used to it by now, but the sheer scale of the Saray Institution made it impossible to be anything other than overwhelmed. The hands of fifty children reached towards us, desperate for attention and hugs.

Dressed in bedclothes and rags, some had shaven heads, giving them the appearance of convicts rather than patients. Everywhere, children exhibited the awful violent rocking of the institutionalised. One of the aid workers told us that the children had been abandoned by their parents and kept in Saray since they were toddlers.

Sarah tried to play with a boy crouched on the dirty floor. His dull eyes looked towards her, and he smiled and stopped rocking. But as we moved to leave the room, he screamed. And his screams were joined by the screams of all the others. Visibly upset, the Duchess bit her bottom lip. Walking away is the most difficult thing to do.

The building seemed to go on for ever. We came across room after room filled with children, all equally desperate for attention. As I left one area, I nearly tripped over a boy lying on his back in the middle of the corridor, his face in a shaft of sunlight. One of the carers hastily moved him back into the room, explaining that he often crawled out towards the window in the corridor just to feel the sun on his face. I found it almost unbearably sad. 'Most of the children never go outside,' the carer added. 'There are too many of them for us to handle.'

The complex was so vast that we had to travel to the next building by car. On arrival, a care worker tried to usher us past a set of imposing double doors. I could hear the cries of children from behind them, and asked to go inside. The worker took some persuasion before eventually relenting, and it soon became clear why. Before us was a sea of red and blue cribs – hundreds of them in a huge room. Toddlers and teenagers alike were confined behind metal bars. In a far corner, one little boy peered over the edge of a five foot-high wooden box in which he was kept. According to staff, he was too hyperactive for a crib.

This wasn't an orphanage. It was a warehouse for abandoned children. We spent nearly an hour wandering from crib to crib, trying to take in the awful existence endured by each child. Sarah found thin strips of bed linen scattered on the floor, evidence that some of the children were often tied up. To our horror, the staff began to feed them where they lay: it became clear that the children never leave their confined space, spending all day, every day lying on their backs, even at meal times.

Up to this point, Sarah had remained uncharacteristically quiet, almost as if in shock, but now she appeared furious: 'Look at them, they are just stuffing the food in. Stuffing it in! But it's not their fault. They are wearing janitor uniforms – they're not trained to care for these children. They don't know they are doing wrong.'

MDRI had been told by aid workers that this inhumane process can lead to terrible infections in the back of the mouth, causing appalling pain and suffering.

The Duchess asked how long children stayed in the institution. 'All their lives,' came the reply. 'They never leave.'

The member of staff acting as our guide offered to show us a room where adults were kept. Here, the evidence of poor care was even more conclusive. Many were tied to benches like dogs. Two women sharing a bed covered in faeces jumped to their feet as we entered the room, excited to have visitors. As they turned, they revealed tight bindings around their hands, pinning their arms behind their backs.

The stench was unbearable. Both Sarah and I retched as we watched a woman eat the contents of her nappy. 'She is bored,' explained a worker. 'We cannot change their nappies because we cannot afford to keep buying them.' Suddenly, the worker grew nervous and asked if we were filming. We had pushed our luck to the limit. It was time to leave. Sarah said nothing as we made a hasty departure, her eyes filled with tears. We had spent two hours in Saray, and it had deeply disturbed us both. Our only comfort was the knowledge that soon we would be exposing the conditions there, though we knew it would take great international pressure to tackle such a massive problem.

As we drove away, the Duchess pulled a strip of cloth from her pocket, used to tie up one of the children. 'This is my inspiration,' she said. 'I will take this with me to every speech I make about what we witnessed here.'

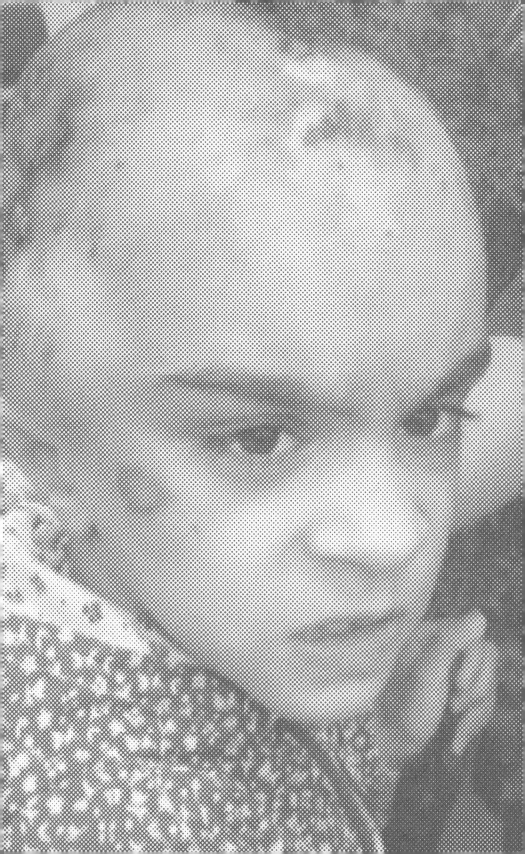

CHAPTER EIGHT

RETURN TO ROMANIA

Turkey's plan to expand the huge Saray Institution did have one positive side – in theory at least. Instead of constructing more appalling human warehouses, it was aiming to follow the Romanian model with dozens of smaller family-type buildings, each housing around fifteen new arrivals cared for by live-in staff.

Romania, our next destination, had already built a staggering two thousand of these smaller homes a few years earlier, announcing with a great fanfare that this showed how much it cared for its abandoned children. When I filmed in several of them in 2006, I was full of hope they would at last provide the loving, supportive environment the children so desperately needed. But sadly, I discovered that bricks and mortar improvements meant little in the absence of proper care. As in many of the larger institutions, the staff were chronically over-worked and under-trained, and conditions for most of the children were as poor as ever.

Romania's response to the fresh wave of criticism had been to promise better training for all staff, while also pledging to continue shutting down its large, old institutions, which had become so notorious for poor care.

Filming in secret with the Duchess – joined this time by Beatrice – we wanted to record what progress had been made in honouring these commitments. As we drove into the capital Bucharest from the airport without delay or drama, I had to pinch myself: another country, another princess – and another journey with no press on our tail. I allowed myself a quiet smile of satisfaction before we got down to what I antici-pated would once again be pretty grim business.

We were heading to one of the worst institutions I had visited two years earlier, Marin Pazon, situated in a back street of Bucharest. It was images from this very orphanage which had first moved the Duchess to get in touch with me, leading to our current filming trip. I assumed Marin Pazon would have been high on Romania's list for closure, so I was shocked to discover that it was still in operation.

A charity which had access to the orphanage told us that fifty-three children were still living there, experiencing what it considered a very poor standard of care. Before the arrival of Sarah and Beatrice, members of our production team briefly visited the orphanage with the charity to check it out and confirm the worst: there had been little improvement in the lives of the remaining children.

Now we needed to get the evidence on tape, but I feared that after my previous high profile reports, I might well be recognised by the staff and blow our cover. I explained to Sarah and Beatrice that the charity would show them round as potential 'donors', but on this occasion they would have to go in without me. We arranged for two members of the *Tonight* production team to secretly film the visit, and confirmed once more that, if the Duchess and the Princess were recognised, they would simply acknowledge their identity.

My absence was less than ideal from an editorial standpoint, but we knew we had few options. Sarah and Beatrice agreed without hesitation: they were fully committed to doing whatever it took to make a success of the filming trip. Sarah was also desperately keen to visit the institution which had so touched her two years previously.

As our minibus headed towards the orphanage, Beatrice appeared to be taking the whole thing in her stride, displaying no nerves about the undercover filming to come. I was keen to brief her and her mother on what to look out for once they got inside Marin Pazon. Our cameraman began to film, but before I even uttered a word, Beatrice leapt straight in: 'Right Chris, we are going to be you now. You need to tell us what you would be looking out for, and what it is that you want us to do.'

Sarah added with a twinkle in her eye: 'We are going to be mini-Chris's!' Their enthusiasm helped greatly in reducing the tension.

'Look behind closed doors,' I advised them. 'There'll be a lot they won't want you to see. Also, examine the children carefully – often physical restraints are hidden under things like jumpers and blankets.'

Remembering the chaotic and upsetting scenes I had witnessed during my previous visit, I hoped against hope that Sarah and Beatrice would find the situation had improved significantly.

*

When they returned an hour later, the looks on their faces said it all: they were devastated. I was disappointed but not surprised at what they found – unlike Turkey, Romania had lost its power to shock me.

As we drove back to our hotel, we watched the secretly filmed footage on a laptop. The hidden camera followed the Duchess and Beatrice into the playground, where they were mobbed by children desperate for human contact. I noticed that since my visit, the playground had been painted in bright colours and new climbing frames had been erected, but it was clear all was still not well with the children, who were rocking and showing other sign of distress.

I recognised most of the children, and saw that there were some new, very young faces too. Beatrice followed my advice, looking for hidden evidence of poor care, and found that under their coats or blankets, many of the children were restrained.

'When I asked the head nurse why they were tied up, she immediately started to untie them,' said Beatrice angrily. 'She clearly knew it was wrong.'

The hidden camera also caught other members of staff rushing around the playground to untie the rest of the tethered children. The head nurse tried to explain the obvious lack of care: 'We really need help with training. All the staff need to be trained on how to help these children.' She appealed to Sarah and Beatrice to donate to the orphanage, completely unaware that she was talking to a duchess and a princess.

Sarah headed inside the building, which again appeared much more pleasant than when I filmed. It was clean and newly-decorated with cartoon characters painted on the walls, but as the hidden camera tracked Sarah's look around, evidence of a lack of decent care continued to emerge. A girl walked down the corridor with her hands tied behind her back, while in the corner of a room a toddler was eating his own nappy – the staff did nothing to stop him.

A nurse was seen on tape admitting that the institution was illegal, explaining to Sarah that they housed one-year-olds to twenty-three-year-olds. Under international and Romanian law, mixing children with adults is illegal, and children under the age of three should not be institutionalised at all.

The staff seemed to be growing suspicious of the team, asking them if they had been given permission by the local authorities to visit the facility, but Sarah pressed on, heading up a flight of stairs to a network of rooms which I hadn't seen on my visit in 2006.

What she found was shocking. Young children were lying alone in cots, and among them was a boy who looked about four years old with an abnormally large head. He had hydrocephalus, or 'water on the brain', and although in many cases it's a treatable condition, nothing had ever been done to help the boy. The nurse told Sarah he was actually eleven years old.

Remembering my briefing, Sarah then demanded that the nurse open up another room that was locked. To her complete horror, she found an emaciated teenage girl called Karina, who had been tied by her hands and ankles to a bed. The staff seemed to find nothing unusual in this treatment, casually explaining that she was kept tied up like this for at least four hours every day to 'keep her calm'.

As we watched back the appalling images in our minibus, Sarah was clearly still furious: 'What says it all is that they called it therapy. Karina must be twelve or thirteen, and I saw a doctor push his hands down her nappy to see if she had filled it. A telling sign is that Karina doesn't even seem to mind – it's all she has known.'

The footage then showed the Duchess almost blowing the team's cover as she demanded that Karina be untied. Despite insisting that the tying up of children was not wrong, the nurse bowed to the pressure and agreed to free her. But before she had a chance to do so, the Duchess impatiently began to untie Karina herself.

At first, this sat uncomfortably with me. As a reporter I always avoid getting actively involved in this way – unless it's an immediate matter of life and death. No matter how tough I find it on occasion not to intervene, I always remind myself that I'm there to tell a story, not to become part of it.

But I couldn't be angry with Sarah. The footage demonstrated that she is an impassioned humanitarian who will never settle for merely being a witness like me. Nevertheless, as I had feared, her actions jeopardised the secret mission. One of the staff asked the team directly if they were journalists, forcing the team to beat a hasty retreat.

I closed my laptop, and everyone in the vehicle fell into an uneasy silence. It was one of those increasingly common occasions during my investigations when I found my emotions all over the place. The journalist in me wanted to congratulate the whole team on some amazing secret footage, but I was so revolted by what I'd just seen that it seemed completely inappropriate.

Once again, Beatrice was showing great strength and maturity: 'What they need is support. They need experts to help them learn how to give the children the right physiotherapy. The head nurse thinks she is doing the best job she can, but the reality is that she is completely overwhelmed.'

'You're absolutely right, Beatrice,' I responded, 'and they will promise to train and educate these workers when this is exposed, like they do every time. But unfortunately they never do anything.'

*

For a country that kept insisting it had reformed its child welfare system, we could have been forgiven for assuming Marin Pazon was an isolated case. But sadly, according to aid workers, it was anything but. To prove this we were taken to another large institution in Bucharest where, in room after room, we found similar neglect and lack of care.

And as we were taken up the stairs to a different area, we were greeted with a disturbing situation I hadn't seen before. There were more than eighty children crammed in to one small room in stifling heat. Their carers claimed they were living and sleeping in the area as a temporary measure while other parts of the building were being refurbished. We were told the youngest was two, the eldest ten. They looked like a carpet of children, sitting crossed-legged in rows on the dirty floor.

But unlike other victims of institutionalisation in the building, they did not rock or show any other signs of distress – they were clearly just extremely bored. We were told they had arrived relatively recently because of a new problem, an unfortunate consequence of Romania's entry into the European Union.

'They have been abandoned by parents who have left the country to find work in other EU countries,' explained a carer. 'Some children may eventually go back home – but only if their parents ever come back'. The carer pointed to a blonde boy who looked about eight years old. 'He has been waiting for over a year, and we are struggling to find foster families for them all.'

Experts later told us that it takes just eighteen months in institutional care for the classic physical and emotional effects to begin to show – much longer than that and the damage is usually permanent.

To the delight of the children, Sarah insisted on reading a story to them and singing some songs. It was a surreal moment for an undercover news operation, but it summed up what I liked about working with the Duchess. We had become quite a unique team: while I was passionate to expose the issues, she was equally passionate to bring help, even with the smallest of acts.

*

Given the great number of smaller, family-type homes across Romania, we completed our investigations by seeing if the level of care in these had improved – as promised by the authorities after my last undercover filming trip. Having gained access to one home by posing as aid workers, we found that there were still nowhere near enough trained staff, with just one carer and one cook for nine children. While there was no evidence of children actually tied up on this occasion, they seemed neglected and distressed, with many endlessly rocking back and forth. We even witnessed one young boy left rocking on the toilet on his own for over half an hour.

It was all, unfortunately, as I had predicted, and we came away deeply depressed. Sarah and Beatrice desperately needed to see a project which was succeeding, and I knew just the place to lift their spirits. I took them to the outskirts of Oradea in the north west of the country to meet British aid worker Sarah Wade, who had built her own version of family-type homes through her charity Romanian Relief.

Two homes housed a total of twelve children, who she had rescued from State care. She refused to call the homes 'orphanages' or 'institutions', and with good reason: Romanian carers fostered the children and brought them up as their own, and local, highly-trained nurses carried out daily therapy in a specially-built room.

Before we stepped inside, Sarah Wade explained that there was one particular child she wanted us to meet. 'Her name is Lydia, and she is the greatest inspiration of them all. I found her when she was seven years old, battered and bruised in a State orphanage.'

She handed us a photograph of Lydia, taken the day of her rescue. The Duchess and Beatrice were clearly appalled by what they saw – Lydia was bald and her face and head were covered in bruises and scars.

'She was tied up in a cot in a tiny room with other children,' explained Sarah Wade. 'As an aid worker I was only allowed to spend short periods of time with her and the other children, to give them some company. That was it, that was all the staff would allow me to do. When I left, the children would scream. Eventually I began to untie Lydia while I was with her. At first, she would punch or knee her own face – she was very disturbed. But I could see that with trust and plenty of love, she would stop abusing herself.'

As we walked into the garden of the Romanian Relief home, Lydia ran into Beatrice's arms and dragged her away to play on the swings. Four years on, she was a girl transformed: a happy, healthy child with long brown hair and a pretty face.

'Most of the children were in a terrible state when they arrived,' said Sarah Wade, 'mainly from physiological and physical problems that developed while they were under State care. Now they are in a home full of love and care.'

The family atmosphere, the laughter and the fun were all something we took for granted back home, but here, after everything we'd seen elsewhere in Romania, they represented something very special which clearly touched the Duchess. 'I am moved and inspired by this home. In Marin Pazon I was left passionate to do something about Karina and the other children, but the care of these people here has moved my heart.'

Sarah and Beatrice played with the children for hours. Beatrice looked very much at home, perhaps the most comfortable I had seen her. It was obviously a welcome relief from the horrors of the last few days and, more importantly, it had shown the young Princess that there is hope in almost all situations, no matter how terrible.

'There is something completely unique and special about this place,' she observed. 'I really like the idea that Romania is helping Romania by bringing in foster parents and therapists from the local community. It's so special that it's something more people should copy.'

Just like her younger sister, Beatrice had been left desperate to create change after all she had seen. And just like her mother, she thought big: 'Wouldn't it be great if we could actually stop the need for places like this! Why should children be abandoned in the first place? We should try and stop that.'

'I am with Beatrice on this one,' added her mother. 'I think I would be dishonouring you, Chris, if I came here with you and didn't find a solution. I couldn't see abhorrent sights and not back it up; I'm just not that sort of person. I cannot make false promises – as Mary Poppins said: "a pie-crust promise, easily made and easily broken" – I'm not about pie-crust promises.'

*

Sarah Wade suggested I take the Duchess and the Princess to witness one of the root causes of Romania's problems. As I had seen on my previous visit, Romanian Relief were working hard in a gypsy village called

Tinca, supporting mothers in an attempt to stop them abandoning their children. But it had been a real struggle battling against the Third World conditions. With no electricity or clean water, and with little work, desperate mothers had few options. That very week, the Romanian Relief team had counted eighteen abandoned babies in the local maternity hospital, many of them from Tinca, and we were told the numbers were almost certainly going to rise as winter approached.

We were introduced to Maritza, one of the mothers who had abandoned her baby. She looked emotional and exhausted, with a dirty face and ragged clothes. Nevertheless, she didn't hesitate in inviting us into her wooden shack. As we sat down, she explained that she was also about to abandon two of her older children, both aged two.

Like most visitors to the village, including myself, the Duchess initially found this very hard to comprehend: 'So you would rather put your children in an institution than have them here at home with you?'

'What mother does not love her children?' replied Maritza, as she picked up one of the two-year-olds and began sobbing.

'You clearly love your children so much,' said Sarah, shaking her head in disbelief at what she was witnessing. 'They are getting so much love from you. Nothing compares to a mother's love.'

Maritza grabbed the Duchess's hand. 'Yes, I can give them love, but what else? No home, no food, no heat, no help.'

Sarah's eyes filled up as she realised Maritza's awful predicament. 'This is an impossible situation, just impossible,' she said.

It hadn't escaped Sarah that some of the mothers in Tinca were actually much younger than her own daughters. I arranged for Beatrice to meet Maria, a fifteen-year-old who was about to have her third child. As we walked towards her shack, two children clothed in rags ran towards Beatrice and cuddled up to her. Beatrice looked upset and pleaded with their young mother: 'Please tell me these children are not going to be abandoned.' 'I desperately want to keep my babies,' Maria told Beatrice. 'My heart will bleed if I have to abandon them.' But the heavily pregnant teenager confirmed the worst: 'I feel it's a mercy for my children to be institutionalised. I have no choice, they deserve a proper home.'

The overwhelming desperation of the young mothers was something I had filmed many times before, a crucial piece of the jigsaw in understanding the cycle of abandonment. But once again, Sarah brought something unique to this filming trip. As I watched her hold the hands of tearful mothers or cradle their starving children, it became clear she shared something with them that I could never offer – the universal compassion of mothers.

'It's all so easy to ask: "Why did they abandon a child?"' said Sarah. 'I couldn't imagine in a million years abandoning Beatrice and Eugenie, so you immediately think they must be bad mothers. But no, I have seen that's not the case. You have to imagine that you cannot provide a roof for your child, who is starving and freezing to death. Then you understand why they end up leaving them in a hospital or institution. What they don't know is that by doing so, they are handing them a death sentence.'

Our visit to Tinca was a turning point in Sarah's ambition to bring help to Romania's children. This was the moment she realised exactly what she wanted to do. 'We cannot stamp out poverty, but as a mother – not some fuddy-duddy Duchess – I will bring them support and help so they keep their kids. This is my cause.'

Beatrice was equally moved to help: 'When the children grabbed me and wanted me to hold them, I found myself looking into their eyes and wanting desperately to do something. Just one loving look and I became a part of this situation.'

Both knew that helping mothers keep their children was also the key to relieving pressure on the State institutions. 'My first impression as we arrived in the village was overwhelming,' said Beatrice, 'but as time went on it became a lot easier to understand. There is a cycle here and to make a difference you have to break the cycle. I have found my mission in life now. This is it: it's Tinca, then the next village!'

The camera crew and I left Sarah and Beatrice to wander the dirt tracks of the village alone, taking in the poverty around them and the enormous task ahead of them.

*

It was our last night in Romania. Over dinner, the Duchess and Beatrice devised a plan with Sarah Wade and her staff to change the lives of every mother in Tinca. Together, they calculated the costs of fitting out an existing building as a clinic and community centre which would provide family planning advice, medical support and childcare. A new wing would act as an emergency centre to provide beds, food and warmth during the toughest months.

As I watched them full of enthusiasm around the table, drawing sketches of different designs, I felt proud to have played my part in bringing them all together to help transform so many lives. But knowing the British press and their relationship with the Duchess, it also occurred to me that some papers would probably look for a negative angle, perhaps accusing her of doing it for self-publicity. I asked the Duchess if this worried her.

'Those cynics should sweep their side of the street,' was her uncompromising response. 'Have they done anything today? Did they bring a smile to someone's face? Were they kind and nice? Before they make judgements on other people, perhaps they need to look at themselves first.'

The undercover filming trips had been far more successful than I had dared believe possible. I was heading home with shocking images of poor care in two countries, both of which had previously promised radical change – and all with a duchess and two princesses as eyewitnesses. Their involvement would guarantee maximum attention for the issues, but nothing could have prepared us for the controversy that awaited us on our return to Britain.

CHAPTER NINE

CHILDREN SHOULD BE SEEN
AND NOT HURT

Detailed accounts of our investigation and copies of our secretly filmed footage were sent to the Turkish and Romanian governments, so they had a chance to give their reactions to our findings.

Typically, I would have expected to receive a written statement, but perhaps with the seriousness of the accusations and the likely global attention in mind, both countries decided to send representatives to London to be interviewed.

In order to do full justice to these government responses, ITV executives commissioned a second thirty minute edition of the *Tonight* programme, to be broadcast the night after the one hour documentary.

The production team couldn't have been more delighted: two prime-time slots focussing on the issue.

After all the terrible things we had witnessed, I relished the prospect of confronting the two governments face to face with our evidence. The interviews were to prove some of the most extraordinary I have conducted in my career.

With a week to go to broadcast, we entered the grand reception room in the Turkish Embassy to be met by a large crowd of stony-faced officials. Recep Dogan introduced himself grandiloquently as the 'legal advisor and representative of the General Directorate of the Turkish Social Services and Child Protection Agency'.

As we set up the cameras and lights, he paced the floor of the room looking nervous and highly-strung. I prepared myself for an awkward interview.

His opening gambit was completely unexpected; as he took his seat he insisted on reading out a detailed statement on camera:

> We should not forget that these institutions are
> not orphanages: they are institutions for the
> mentally disabled. Any person who has tiny wisdom
> and consciousness can understand that. Disabled
> people behave the same way in institutions
> everywhere including the United Kingdom. But we
> take the allegations seriously.
>
> Many international organisations including
> the Council of Europe have expressed their
> satisfaction about our institutions. Our
> institutions will always be open to non-
> governmental organisations and experts. We know
> that some of our institutions need refurbishment
> and renovation.

Then, out of the blue, came a serious threat: 'We highly believe that we have a very strong argument to stop your broadcast of your film by applying to the High Court and getting an injunction. Therefore, we reserve our right to go to court.'

If an injunction were applied for, the broadcast of the film would have to be suspended until the High Court made a decision. It could take a few days, weeks or even months. We immediately stopped filming, and the producer left the Embassy to call the ITV lawyer for advice.

Despite his threat of legal action, Mr Dogan agreed to answer specific questions in relation to our findings. Having got a green light from our lawyer to continue, I began by pointing out that we had seen – and filmed – a huge number of children in institutions showing classic signs of institutionalisation, including rocking and self-harm.

Mr Dogan took a different view of such behaviour: 'This is a general characteristic of the mentally disabled,' he claimed. 'It has nothing to do with institutionalising them. We are taking every possible measure to avoid the effects of institutionalisation. We are providing lots of activities for them both inside and outside a complex.'

'So, for example, why did we find a boy on the floor in Saray who crawled to the window to feel the sunlight because he never goes outside?' I asked.

Mr Dogan again put this down to disability: 'This child is totally mentally and physically disabled. He's getting sunshine and he likes it – but I agree he should not have been left unsupervised.'

It was not just the effects of institutionalisation that Mr Dogan refused to accept; he also denied the very existence of some of the children we filmed, such as the girl in Zeytinburnu who was restrained by her jumper and left alone on the floor. When I asked him for a response to even worse treatment in Saray, where we filmed dozens of children and adults tied up, he insisted – against all our eyewitness and taped evidence – that there were only two children tethered, adding that: 'one of them was tied up from behind because he was a risk to himself and the other children.'

Mr Dogan did not deny the existence of the little boy we filmed confined to a wooden box, but stated there was nothing wrong with his care: 'He is kept there for his own protection – and the box was specially made for him.'

'Why are other children being confined to cots in Saray and fed lying down?' I asked. But he was becoming increasingly agitated by my questioning, and at this point decided attack was the best form of defence.

'You didn't get consent of the children to film them. This is very important,' he shouted.

'Well, it's in the public interest,' I replied, attempting to remain calm. I couldn't believe he had the nerve to try to turn the tables, and claim we were the ones not taking care of the children's welfare.

'There is no public interest,' he asserted.

'Believe me, Mr Dogan, there's a lot of public interest in how these children are cared for, especially in a country that wants to be a member of the European Union ... '

'You could have protected the interests of the children by not filming,' he interrupted me angrily.

'Is Turkey protecting the interests of physically and mentally disabled children?' I responded.

'Of course we are,' replied a defiant Mr Dogan.

'By tying them up? Confining them to cribs? And feeding them lying down?'

In the face of our overwhelming evidence, he finally admitted all was not perfect: 'I accept you found irregularities and we need to train our staff. This is not just to be in the European Union. We will do this because we want to, for our children.'

'And the Duchess of York wants to help you,' I told him. 'She wants to work with you, not against you.'

'We did not invite the Duchess of York. We did not ask for her help or her money. Who invited her?'

*

As with any investigation, we had shown our footage to various leading figures for their expert opinion on the findings. The reaction from top human rights barrister, John Cooper, made an interesting comparison with Turkey's interpretation of the documentary. 'The footage you have shown me is Dickensian,' said John with some disgust, 'and quite frankly that's an insult to Charles Dickens. That a child has to crawl along the floor to obtain sunlight is shocking. You don't need to be a human rights expert to see that that must be in contravention of fundamental human dignity, let alone a legal statute.

'There is also quite clearly psychological disturbance – one doesn't need to be trained in psychology or psychiatry to see that the young people are not only institutionalised, but disturbed. As for tying people up and restraining them, that is treating them like prisoners.

'When we see this sort of footage, we've got to be very careful where the blame should be apportioned. In my opinion, it's common for the blame to be automatically given to the staff, and that would be wrong. We should look to the State here that has woefully failed to support their staff in looking after their people – I would guess that a lot of the staff seeing this footage would be just as keen as we are to put things right.

'As I watched the footage I kept thinking that I had seen the worst,' he continued, 'and then I see a child being kept in a box. It flies in the face of United Nations conventions. It flies in the face of the rights of children. It flies in the face of the rights of human dignity and it is clearly in breach of international law.'

I asked John where he felt our footage left the American and British governments' support for Turkey in its bid to join the European Union. He had an unequivocal opinion on this: 'The film shows examples of the way Turkey treats some of its children; the European Union and governments should be taking a very, very firm attitude to what they see in this documentary. Any decent human being would know that a country that treats its children like this is not ready to accede to a family of nations that aspires to dignity and humanity.'

*

Unlike Turkey, Romania said it was keen to discuss the Duchess of York's plans to help abandoned children. So Sarah joined me for the interview with Romania's Secretary of State for Child Welfare, Mariela Neagu, at the Romanian Embassy in London.

I began by reminding Mrs Neagu that we found various breaches of international law in the Bucharest facility Marin Pazon, with toddlers and children institutionalised alongside adults. To my surprise, the Secretary of State made no attempt to deny our findings.

'This is happening because the child welfare departments are struggling to find them foster parents. Our dream is to shut down every single large institution and place unwanted children into family care. The children at Marin Pazon, for example, should have been found foster parents by now. If we don't find families we will put them into the smaller institutions, the family-type homes. It takes time but we are getting there.'

Mrs Neagu's straight talking was refreshing, but when I asked her for a response over the tying up of children, she referred to some astonishing Romanian legislation: 'According to the Health Law in Romania, the tying up of children can take place for up to fours hours a day under certain circumstances, such as extremely violent behaviour, being self-aggressive or aggressive towards others, and it must be done under strict medical supervision.'

'That is a complete breach of international law,' I pointed out. 'You have made promises to improve the care of your children countless times, Mrs Neagu. You promised it as a condition of European Union membership, and before that you yourself actually stated in a report authored by you on Romania's child welfare system: "Romania has proved her commitment to caring for her children." That is absolute rubbish, is it not?'

Once again, the Secretary of State made no attempt to defend Romania's record: 'We do not encourage the restraint of children. I admit those children do not have sufficient qualified staff to look after them. We are trying to make improvements to the system all the time. We are not going to deny that staff are in need of training.'

She turned to the Duchess: 'I would welcome you to return to our institutions and help us to find ways to improve the lives of children.'

'That's great,' replied Sarah, seizing the opportunity. 'This is what I want to hear; I am not here for a fight. You are a mother and I am a mother. Together we can work towards solutions. I will do whatever it takes to be able to hear that Karina, the girl who I found tied to her bed, and other children like her are now able to enjoy their childhood. Let's make this happen.'

I was heartened by Mrs Neagu's humility in asking for the help of the Duchess, and came away feeling the interview was a definite turning point in the attitude of the Romanian government. But after so many false dawns, I still reserved judgement on whether it would be translated into significant improvements in the life of abandoned children.

I was also shocked that Romania had passed a law which allowed the tying up of children. When I showed barrister John Cooper the footage of tethered children in Romanian institutions, he shared my concerns.

'A restraint is categorically outlawed – even the restraint of juveniles in prisons and youth offender institutions, be that in Romania, Turkey or the United Kingdom. Restraint of young people is only a final resort and even then it is frowned upon. The restraint of children with special needs is absolutely and utterly unacceptable. It is illegal and they know it.'

SUNDAY 2ND NOVEMBER 2008 – FOUR DAYS TO TRANSMISSION

The public's first glimpse of the Duchess's secret mission came in a two page article I wrote for the British newspaper, the *Mail on Sunday*. The reaction was immediate and overwhelming: thousands of emails and messages were posted on the newspaper's website by readers from around the world, expressing shock at the appalling conditions endured by abandoned children – and praise for Sarah for sticking her neck out.

As other reporters picked up on the story, my phone rang almost constantly with interview requests. By early evening, ITV was running the first trails for the documentary, and the number of calls from journalists reached a peak. All were anxious to get more details from me before their deadlines. I couldn't sleep that night, knowing that the next day the story would dominate newspapers across the globe.

MONDAY 3RD NOVEMBER 2008 – THREE DAYS TO TRANSMISSION

When you wake up at seven a.m. to thirty missed calls on your mobile, you know you are in for a turbulent day. Most of the messages were from Turkish journalists, bidding for interviews about the documentary. I called the ITV press office and they confirmed that banner headlines were splashed across the Turkish press, expressing their horror at what we had found:

'Turkey will be shamed'

… proclaimed one, while another wrote:

'The world will see these pictures!'

Others quoted my article, using lines such as:

'The Duchess's eyes filled with tears for Turkey's Children'

and

'Tied like pets to benches.'

In the UK, pictures of Eugenie sobbing outside the Istanbul orphanage had been released to the press, and the image was carried by nearly every British paper, with very similar headlines along the lines of

'Eugenie's Tears for Turkey's Orphans.'

Later that evening, Turkey's prime-time news programmes broadcast our footage of the Zeytinburnu and Saray Institutions without permission from ITV. We could only assume that the material we had sent to the government had been leaked to the media – Turkish ministers accused ITV of doing the same.

But that wasn't the only accusation that came from the Turkish government. Leading the charge, Nimet Cubukcu, the State Minister responsible for the Social Services and Child Protection, made a ridiculous statement accusing the Duchess of a politically motivated campaign against Turkey.

'The bad intent behind the film was most obvious,' Ms Cubukcu told a reporter, referring to the imminent publication of a new report from the European Union on Turkey's progress as a candidate for membership. While nobody in our production team had any idea this rather specialised report was due, Ms Cubukcu was apparently convinced the timing was deliberate.

'It was known that this Sarah was against Turkey's EU bid,' she asserted bizarrely. 'She has run a campaign against Turkey's membership of the European Union.'

The Minister failed to comment on our images of children tied up, fed lying down and confined to cots without proper care. But the tide was about to turn on a government that appeared to be in denial.

TUESDAY 4TH NOVEMBER 2008 – TWO DAYS TO TRANSMISSION

'Duchess Accused of Smear Campaign against Turkey!' ... was typical of the stories now being run by newspapers around the world. It was not ideal – we would far rather have seen headlines referring to the real issue of mistreatment of children – but on the plus side, Turkey had helped fuel press interest with its denials, so images and key findings from the documentary were also being seen globally, from Europe to America, Canada, South Africa and Australia. It was even headline news in China and Japan.

The Turkish media was now referring to the documentary as 'The Duchess Crisis'. Speaking about the 'crisis' on a number of news programmes, Ali Babacan, the Foreign Minister, criticised the way the film was made using hidden cameras, claiming it was 'a breach of privacy'. Like his ministerial colleague the day before, he failed to make any reference to the negligent care of children revealed in the documentary.

Instead, the Turkish government released its own footage of the Zeytinburnu Institution in Istanbul, showing happy children in a clean and friendly environment. But it was something of an own goal, with the country's media responding that 'the authorities had ordered a clean-up of Istanbul orphanages after reports about the film surfaced', and pointing out that 'the footage was not independently filmed'.

Pressure was coming from Turkey's own people to give a more credible reaction, with opposition politicians, observers and experts emerging in a number of newspapers, and even on special television debates about the film.

'Since they came to power, for many years the government has known about the problems exposed by the British reporter and the Duchess,' claimed an opposition Minister. Perhaps alluding to the MDRI report, he went on: 'Violence and poor conditions in Turkish orphanages were exposed by experts long before the Duchess's visit – why has nothing been done?'

One of the country's leading child psychiatrists complained that bad conditions and a lack of staff were not confined to the institutions we had visited.

'Conditions in all children's homes in Turkey are very bad,' the expert told the *Radikal* newspaper. 'There is a lack of resources, infrastructure and personnel.' On another debate programme, a brave former worker at the Saray Institution dared to speak out, confirming that there was 'a horrific lack of care', and that she and other workers 'had no idea what to do for the children'.

WEDNESDAY 5TH NOVEMBER 2008 – ONE DAY TO TRANSMISSION

It was nine a.m. and I was in a reflective mood, sitting alone in a large press conference room at the headquarters of ITV. I glanced at the large screen on which would soon be showing the film that few thought we would pull off, with a woman and her daughters at my side that few thought would see it through.

Often when my work is about to be shown, I feel great pride, but on this occasion it was more a genuine sense of satisfaction: the last few months of sheer slog and worry seemed completely worthwhile.

As the room began to fill with journalists and camera crews, I slipped away to greet the Duchess and Princess Beatrice (her sister Eugenie was working abroad with her father, Prince Andrew). You would think the prospect of a press conference would be daunting for any twenty-year-old, but Beatrice was beaming with confidence.

However, I knew Sarah well enough to see she was a bag of nerves, and it struck me that it was because she was about to face the British press. I found it hard to imagine what that must be like for her, when over so many years they had rarely had a good word to say about her – whatever she did. Now, of course, they were lapping up the political storm around her involvement in the filming.

After working so closely with Sarah, I came to realise that she doesn't care about negative headlines: it's being misunderstood that gets under her skin. As we headed into the lion's den, I knew she needed some reassurance: 'If nobody takes any notice of our findings, if there is a wall of silence from the governments responsible, then we have achieved nothing,' I told her. 'We have created debate and anger and that means we have created change. That is the glorious side effect of what we have done.' Sarah smiled and winked at me. We took our seats under the watchful eye of the press, the lights dimmed and the documentary began.

There was an awkward silence as the one hour film ended; some journalists were clearly moved by our findings. But depressingly, it seemed several tabloid reporters had been sent not to report on the shocking contents of the documentary, but to find, as ever, a negative story to write about Sarah.

They threw in the obvious questions about her motives, and asked for reaction to the accusations of the Turkish government that she had 'launched a smear campaign.' Sarah was unfazed: 'I am apolitical and multi-faith, and nobody would be more pleased than me if Turkey does eventually join the European Union. That may of course surprise the Turkish government, who strangely seem to believe I have the will – and the power – to destroy their political ambitions. But if and when they do join the EU, it will mean the country has adhered to all the conditions set for membership, including improving its human rights record. On that day, there should not be a single child tethered and left in the darkness of an institution.'

'Is helping to expose humanitarian issues something a member of the Royal family should be doing?' a reporter asked Beatrice. Her response would become a headline in many newspapers the following day: 'There is more to Royalty than cutting ribbons.'

In interviews with television news journalists, Sarah spoke from the heart: 'I went as a mum, and I went because those children are silent whispers. Today, I am not speaking for Sarah Ferguson, I am speaking for Max who is kept in a box, and for a boy who crawls to the window just to feel sunlight because he never goes outside, and for Karina who is tied to her bed because nurses don't know how else to care for her needs. And quite frankly, I'm very proud to stand by that film.'

THURSDAY 6TH NOVEMBER 2008 – TRANSMISSION DAY

It was a timely announcement we hadn't expected: the Foreign Secretary David Miliband and his Turkish counterpart Ali Babacan were to hold a joint press conference in London on Friday, the morning after the broadcast of the documentary. Apparently, talks between the two had been scheduled for many weeks, but now the documentary's findings would dominate the agenda.

The press conference would make a significant, last minute element for the second programme. To make sure of it, I requested a pass for myself and a film crew to attend the briefing, but the British Foreign Office initially insisted only Turkish press were allowed to attend. A ban on British press was both astonishing and unheard of. We threatened to mention it in the programme, and an hour later I received a call from the Foreign Office insisting that it had been a misunderstanding – ITV were of course welcome.

In an eleventh hour bid, the Turkish authorities once again appealed to ITV to cancel the broadcast of the film; if not, they claimed they would apply for a High Court injunction. The threat had been a dark cloud hanging over the entire production team, but with just hours to go to broadcast, it now seemed nothing more than intimidation.

At nine p.m., the *Tonight Special: Duchess and Daughters: Their Secret Mission* was broadcast on ITV1. I knew every shot and every word of my commentary, but felt drawn to watch it all again – no matter how often you see a programme, for some strange reason it always feels different catching it as it's going out.

As the documentary drew to a close, I felt an overwhelming sense of relief. I also found myself thinking back to that first meeting with the Duchess in a hotel room, and how, deep down, I had honestly never dreamt we would actually make it all happen.

FRIDAY 7TH NOVEMBER 2008 – BROADCAST OF SECOND PROGRAMME

I was disappointed to find that reviews of the documentary in some newspapers seemed more concerned about questioning the Duchess's involvement in the documentary, rather than reflecting on the exposure of such gross injustice to young children. But I was gratified by other coverage, particularly in *The Independent*:

'These children should be seen and not hurt'

… was the headline of a review of the film, which went on to comment that: 'The real problem being exposed here was not the institutions themselves, but the surrounding culture, which treats disability as something shameful, to be hidden.' The article concluded pertinently: 'Changing that culture is far beyond the scope even of a princess – or two.'

Our hope was that people with the power to create such fundamental change had been influenced by the documentary. The Foreign Secretary's press conference that morning would be a first chance to test the temperature. As we set up our camera in the Foreign Office, a huge pack of Turkish journalists, photographers and camera crews surrounded me for comment; it felt a little disorientating, as if the hunter had suddenly become the hunted.

I was saved by the prompt entrance of David Miliband and the Turkish Foreign Minister, Ali Babacan. Mr Miliband began by stating that the *Tonight* programme had dominated their scheduled talks. He turned to Mr Babacan and said: 'The ITV documentary is an independent programme and Sarah Ferguson is an independent person.'

Attempts to distance the British government from our film ended there. 'We are very concerned by any allegations or television programmes that show abuse of children of any sort,' the Foreign Secretary continued. 'The descriptions in the programme are extremely distressing, and we welcome Turkey's decision for a full inquiry.' After a week of pressure, the Turkish government had at last been forced to act. I couldn't have hoped for a better quote to put into that evening's programme.

More than six million people tuned in to ITV to watch the two special editions of the *Tonight* programme. And over the coming weeks, millions more watched the documentary as it was broadcast in other countries across the globe.

*

Unfortunately, in the immediate aftermath of the broadcast, little changed on the ground in Turkey. The Turkish government's assurances that it would hold an inquiry into its orphanages turned out to be more of a witch-hunt to root out those deemed responsible for allowing us to film. Many aid workers and charities doing invaluable work were thrown out. Without permission to bring direct help to Turkey's children, the Duchess of York reluctantly settled for the awareness that had been created by the *Tonight* programmes.

The attacks on the documentary also rumbled on, with the Turkish authorities investigating the possibility of the arrest of myself, the Duchess and key members of the production team for trespass on orphanage territory and filming without permission. Feeble as the accusations seemed, Sarah and I found it very unsettling. Turkey even involved the European police agency Interpol, and it was hard to be absolutely sure how far such an unprecedented case could go.

Romania was a completely different story. Inch by inch, things continued to improve on several fronts. Serious training of institution staff was instigated, as promised by the Secretary of State; and crucially, life began to change for many mothers in Romanian gypsy villages, including the village of Tinca which we visited with Sarah and Beatrice.

The ambitious new clinic, planned by the Duchess and the Romanian Relief charity, is gradually taking shape and its services are reaching out to the families in Tinca. Two of the mothers we filmed typify the change.

Soon after we left, Maritza's flimsy shack collapsed, leaving her and her two children homeless. Their fate in the country's institutions would have been sealed, but instead, Romanian Relief were able to provide her with clothes, food and medical care, and, using extra funds donated by the Duchess, move the family into a new home.

The pregnant fifteen-year-old, Maria, gave birth to a baby girl. As she had told us, she planned to abandon her baby on the maternity ward with her two other toddlers. But after counselling and support from the clinic, she changed her mind and decided to keep all her children.

Similar clinics are planned all over Romania, most of them funded by charities. But in a highly significant development, the Romanian government has also adopted the idea, announcing plans to provide more mother and baby units to gypsy communities as a positive alternative to institutionalisation.

But where is the hope for countless other institutionalised children across Europe? Abusive and negligent care has been reported in Bulgaria, Bosnia, Serbia, Kosovo, Albania, Hungary, Czech Republic, Ukraine and Moldova, to name but a few. The scale of the problem remains overwhelming, but if Romania – notorious for so long for its poor care – continues to lead the way in putting its house in order, then other countries may hopefully be inspired to follow.

In the meantime, much of the burden of care rests as ever on the dedication and determination of local staff, charities and aid workers. Long after journalists have packed up their filming equipment and got their story, aid workers continue the struggle to help the vulnerable, whatever the obstacles put in their way by uncaring or corrupt governments.

It's a humanitarian tragedy that the Duchess of York has vowed to dedicate her life's work to, and along the way other influential women have been inspired to help too. A couple of years ago, the American model and actress Lisa B also asked me to take her on one of my trips to Romania, so she could see the situation for herself. I had no idea how much that trip had moved her until she called me around the time of the *Tonight Special*, revealing an idea she had been working on for two years.

'It's called Mothers4Children. I am going to harness the universal compassion of mothers to help not just Romanian children; we are going to reach out to every country we can. It's a philanthropic co-operative – effectively a charity of charities.'

Her campaign was to be led by a rather special source of mum power – an executive committee of famous women. There were pop stars such as Louise Rednapp and Mica Paris, TV presenters including Tess Daley, Trinny Woodall and Anthea Turner, actress Tina Hobley, UNICEF ambassador Jemima Khan and models like Yasmin Le Bon. Lisa appealed for all mothers, famous or not, to join the movement.

At the press launch – on Mothers' Day 2009 at the Mayfair Hotel in London – it was inspiring to see nearly two hundred high profile, powerful women in one room, giving thousands of abandoned children a voice and hope. Singer Louise Rednapp summed up the spirit of the movement.

'I think mothers have to look out for other mothers and other mothers' children,' she told a reporter. 'Someone said to me that when you become a mum you join a club, and I thought: "Yeah right!" But it's true – when I saw the investigation in Romania, I felt helpless until Mothers4Children happened. Together as mums we can make a difference.'

*

Around the same time, fifteen hundred miles away, the spirit of motherhood finally began to bring a glimmer of hope to Turkey's most vulnerable children. It came in the form of a new Turkish politician, Selma Aliye Kavaf, who replaced Nimet Cubukcu, the government minister responsible for the Social Services and Child Protection (and the minister who had accused the Duchess of a smear campaign).

Mrs Kavaf gave an impassioned mission statement when she took up the role: 'I am a woman and a mother. Now all those children who are being taken care of at State facilities are my children. I will do my best to serve the people who need special care. We are here to serve the public. To have this or that title is not important to me in serving this country; the important thing for me is to do my best.'

While fine words are the stock-in-trade of many a politician – and so much is often lost in the translation into action – one can only hope the appointment of Mrs Kavaf represents a genuine turning point.

Sadly, at the time of writing, the Turkish government has still not officially accepted the findings of the ITV documentary. On the contrary, it has persisted in its unlikely campaign to have Sarah and me extradited under Turkish 'privacy' laws. For Turkey to try to prosecute us, rather than admit to its failings in caring for some of its most vulnerable children, is shameful, a crude attempt to divert attention from our disturbing evidence.

Even so, I cannot pretend that such pressure is easy to deal with, especially when it draws in other family members. In mid-November 2009, I was on assignment abroad when I got a call from my wife, Alexis. My heart missed a beat: it was the early hours of the morning and could only be bad news. Her voice was trembling with fear: 'Chris, there are two men in suits outside. They've been banging on the door for the past hour. What do I do?' Alone inside our isolated country cottage, she was terrified.

I felt helpless but tried to calm her down, telling her to sit tight and not let them in. While I spoke to her on her mobile, our home phone rang. It was one of the men outside, and he explained that he was from a special international branch of Scotland Yard on a mission to deliver papers from a Turkish private prosecutor, the first step towards my extradition for trial in Turkey. Later, he apologised for the completely unnecessary trauma he and his colleague had caused Alexis.

Sarah Ferguson's solicitors received a similar letter the same day. The message sent to me and the Duchess by Turkey was clear: if you want to expose our human rights' abuses, there is a price to pay. Turkey's action also led to great pressure on Sarah and me not to go ahead with the publication of this book. But I felt it was important to stand up to these bully-boy tactics for many reasons.

For one, this was a fight for the freedom of the press we are blessed with in the UK. Journalists cannot pursue the truth without the licence to act in the interests of the public, exposing the scandals or failures of individuals, organisations and governments. And there was of course another, even more important cause: to give a platform to the million children without a voice in sub-standard institutions around Europe. Improving the life of any one of those children would have justified our efforts – together they represented a million reasons why we had to continue to fight the establishment.

Inevitably, the press continued to run with the extradition story, finding headlines such as 'Fergie To Be Arrested' and 'Fergie Faces Five Years in Turkish Jail' too good to miss – for better or for worse, the Duchess of York always commands column inches. Not for the first time in her life, Sarah was under intense scrutiny, facing almost unbearable pressure, and I wondered if she perhaps regretted taking part in the film. 'There are days when I think: "Ahhhh! What have I done?"' she admitted. 'But then I think: "No, you have got to come out of a corner now, Sarah; you have got to be who you are meant to be, and stand up with courage for what you think is right." I sort of needed a kick up the backside to get back onto the public stage and be true to myself.

'But what about you?' Sarah asked me. 'What is your inspiration? Why so many investigations on the abandonment of children? Something must have driven you?'

'Well, to be honest it was a story that didn't let go of me, rather than me not letting go of the story,' I told her. Then, for some reason, I went right back to the beginning of my journey, explaining how I came across the horrific orphanage in Sarajevo, while on assignment to report on the alleged apparitions in Medjugorje, ' … and one story on abandoned children simply led to another.'

Sarah's face suddenly lit up: 'Yes, wonderful place, Medjugorje.'

'You've heard of it?' I asked.

'Heard of it? It's extremely special to me! Whatever your faith, whatever your beliefs about that place, you cannot deny something extraordinary is happening there, be it spiritual or something else – Medjugorje inspires incredible journeys in people's lives. Maybe, just maybe, Chris, this was meant to be our journey.'

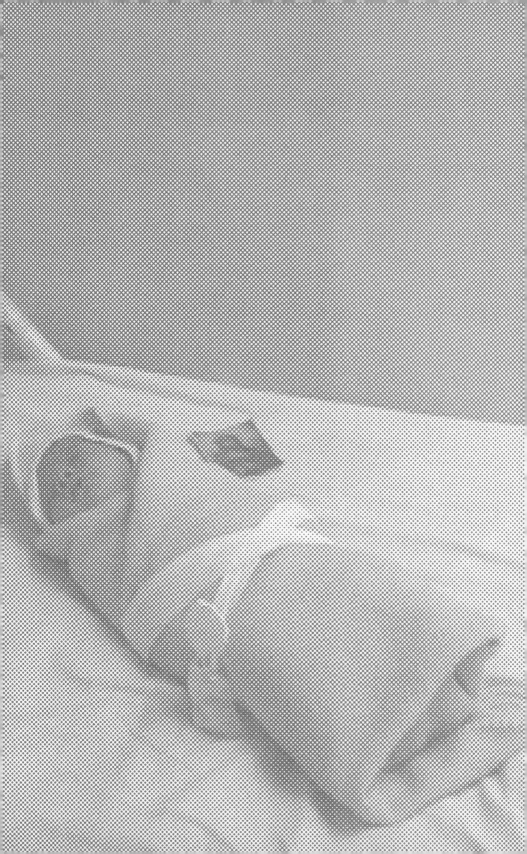

ACKNOWLEDGEMENTS

There is an ITN production and editorial team whose dedication, guidance, faith and experience I am indebted to, especially cameramen Tony Hemmings and Rob Turner, ITV news editor Deborah Turness, ITN lawyer John Battle and all on the Foreign Desk.

I want to pay tribute to the *ITV Tonight* team, especially Mike Lewis, Ruth Gray, Rupert Binsley, Zubin Sarosh, Tom Jennar, Julia Fields and Chris Wissun. Finally the Duchess's team: Rachel Virden, Martin Huberty and Kate Waddington – thank you. Then there is the family, my biggest critics and greatest supporters, Mum, Dad, Gordon, Mary and John – thanks. Alan McCarthy, I hope you are reading this, unknowingly you have played a major role in this story: see Chapter One!

To the aid workers, professionals and individuals who are willing to be named in this book – thank you for your selfless help in my research and filming to bring the plight of abandoned children to the public's attention. Sarah Wade and Ramiz Momeni, as I have always told you, I admire your dedication; you are great aid workers but you would make even better fixers for television news.

Thanks to all at Romanian Relief. Robin Nydes, thank you for your help and for taking twenty calls a day from me for over four years. Branka Boras, thank goodness you didn't change your phone number after a fifteen year gap. You are a true friend who played a huge role in this story; you will not understand how and that is what I admire most about you. Thanks to Jacov too. Nanette Gonzalez, the Brasov gang and Iana Matei, thank you for opening up so many doors for me – you are courageous people. Bob Graham, you are a rare breed of journalist and a terrible driver; thank you for your contacts. To the aid workers, doctors, nurses, social workers and campaigners who cannot be named – and in some cases whose roles cannot be revealed in any capacity in this book – you know who you are and I thank you for your help and loyalty despite the sacrifices, hardship and intimidation you faced.

CHRIS ROGERS
London, December 2009

THE CHARITIES

The purchase of this book has just helped improve the life of an unwanted child – or even saved their life. Funds raised by the sales of *Undercover* will be donated to projects supported by Sarah, the Duchess of York and the charity Mothers4Children.

One of the projects is Romanian Relief's abandonment prevention programme. Funds are desperately needed to help the charity support mothers in the village of Tinca, who may otherwise abandon their children. Romanian Relief believes that to help reduce the rate of abandonment and increase the standard of living within the Roma populations, you must supply basic health care and education. To this end, the charity is working to provide a medical clinic along with daily support from aid workers. The hope is to inspire similar clinics across Romania.

Another beneficiary is a training programme for care workers in institutions. Through its institutional transformation programme, the British charity F.R.O.D.O (Foundation for the Relief of Disabled Orphans) has already trained workers in the Marin Pazon institute in Bucharest. Though the charity abhors institutions and feels that all children should be found a family environment, F.R.O.D.O also feels there is a strong moral obligation not to forget about those left behind. With each month that passes in an institution, the risk of behavioural, cognitive and developmental damage increases dramatically. F.R.O.D.O.'s programme, Institutional Transformation, is designed in conjunction with other experts in the field. Their objective is to work with the staff caring for children in institutions to transform the style and quality of care, resulting in happier, better adjusted children.

MOTHERS4CHILDREN

'When I saw that nothing has changed for these abandoned children, crippled from years confined to a bed I decided I would go to Romania myself as a mum. That trip inspired my charity Mothers4Children. By purchasing this book you will help us reach out to children in need – it should be read by all mothers, it is a story of tragedy and of hope that will inspire you as it did me – Mothers4Children needs you!'

LISA B, MODEL AND ACTRESS
Founder of Mothers4Children

Mothers4Children aims to harness the compassion of women to create a powerful and enduring platform for change. It is more than just a charity; it is a sisterhood of women – mothers, grandmothers, godmothers, daughters, aunts – whose combined mission is to better the lives of all children, because all children deserve love and a great start in life.

M4C is a charity for charities – it identifies and supports existing charitable organisations that have developed successful programmes and services that benefit children in need. The community of M4C aims to provide services, and raise awareness and funds for these projects.

MOTHERS
4 CHILDREN

www.mothers4children.com